Religion and Spirituality

Religion and Spirituality

Eliot Deutsch

1995

STATE UNIVERSITY OF NEW YORK PRESS

Published by
State University of New York Press, Albany

For information, address State University of New York
Press, State University Plaza, Albany, N.Y., 12246

Production by Diane Ganeles
Marketing by Bernadette LaManna

Library of Congress Cataloging-in-Publication Data

Deutsch, Eliot.
    Religion and Spirituality / Eliot Deutsch.
        p.   cm.
    ISBN 0-7914-2457-X (hard : alk. paper). — ISBN 0-7914-2458-8
(pbk. : alk. paper)
    1. Religion—Philosophy. 2. Spirituality. I. Title.
BL51.D415 1995
291.4—dc   94-33771
                                                                    CIP

10 9 8 7 6 5 4 3 2 1

For Marcia

Contents

Preface

I am concerned in this work with the intimate relation—and oftentimes the tension—that obtains between religion and spirituality. Insofar as it involves attention to what we humans take to be sacred, religion has its source and enduring significance, I believe, in spirituality and yet, quite clearly, cannot be identified with it. Also, although religious experience of a relational I-Thou sort is surely a kind of spiritual experience, not all spiritual experience is of that sort. Indeed, much of the profound spirituality of many non-Western philosophical-religious traditions defies characterization in Western personalistic religious terms.

I am not, however, concerned in this work with "religions" as cultural traditions, social/political institutions, or modes of orthopraxy; this is not a work in the "history of religions," valuable and important as that kind of scholarship might be. Nor is it a work in the "philosophy of religion" as usually understood; for although I will discuss from time to time various problems and will address various themes typically associated with this area of philosophy, I will not develop here a sustained argument about issues that have arisen out of Western theism; issues such as the nature and existence of God, the problem of evil, cognitivity in religious belief, faith and reason, and so on—issues which have dominated modern philosophy of religion. This work does not intend to persuade so much as hopefully to call forth and allow a wide range of responses which may awaken one to various possibilities of spiritual experience.

This work includes aphorisms, dialogues, prose-poems, tales, letters, meditations, and even plays, as well as more straightforward analyses. The use of these literary genres— especially the epistolary form—affords, I think, the best opportunity for me to present the varied perspectives that inevitably arise in an exploration of the relations and tensions that obtain between religion and spirituality. Many voices will thus be heard—most of them "authorial"; but I am not trying to hide behind them, disguising thereby my own views or thoughts; rather the employment of these voices seem most naturally to express the varied concerns and possibilities for multi-interpretations that inform this work. Call this, then, if you like, a "postmodern" discourse— but only if this writer's voice is allowed as well to have some- thing essentially to do with the meaning that is inscribed.

Part 1

A Phenomenology of Spirituality

Solitude

Solitude is not a state of withdrawal or of simply being alone; solitude, spiritually, is never only negative in character, a mere turning away, a denial of the social; rather it is—or aspires to be—an enhanced state of being, an achieved state of wholeness, one which makes possible a liberation of consciousness and the attainment of love.

There is a preliminary solitude, an inwardness, which calls for a re-collecting of oneself, a bringing home, as it were, of one's thoughts and memories, one's wayward emotionality and unresolved tensions. Gathering these up, letting them be heard and then re-integrating oneself anew with them is the task of this initial solitude.

There follows the need to "make an island of oneself," a spiritual enclave, but one that is fundamentally different in quality and intensity from that holding back of something of oneself which characterizes so frequently one's relationships with others, however otherwise close or intimate they might be. This need for privacy, in sharp contrast to that which informs spiritual isolation, arises from a fear of self-disclosure and thereby shows a concern for preserving something of oneself that can stand apart from judgement by others. Privacy is a means of self-protection; solitude of self-formation—the attaining to a central integrity of one's being that is free from fear.

This stage of solitude renders one invulnerable to any threat from others, for here one no longer has any little interests of one's own to be challenged. At the same time, however, it renders one completely vulnerable to failure, for if one does not succeed in going beyond this isolation one may very well lose both one's relations with others and oneself.

But why, then, this aloneness with its terrible risk of loss and annihilation? Why not be entirely with others spiritually, say, as a member of a congregation?

The answer: a member of a congregation can relate only to a divinity made personal; warm and comforting as this religious embrace might be, it cannot—indeed does not even aspire to—attain the One.

And so solitude: now become the ground for that "flight of the alone to the alone," one's highest spiritual aspiration.

Spiritual Passivity

Spiritual passivity is the death of the restrictive ego and the birth of true awareness.

Spiritual passivity differs from ordinary passivity insofar as it is a heightened sensitivity and not a simple "waiting to be". It is a presencing of oneself as a person in harmony with being. When liberated by passivity one attains, then, a subtle and expanded attentiveness: one's senses are concentrated; one's feelings are integrated. In the state of spiritual passivity, paradoxically perhaps, one is most free from distractions and one is able thereby to accommodate whatever is.

Spiritual passivity is thus not so much a renouncing of activity as it is a simple letting-go of everything that stands in the way of a solitary communion. In spiritual passivity, *agency*, but not *activity* as such is suspended; which is to say, one is not carrying out some task with a specific end or purpose in view, with means appropriate to it, and so on, but one is very much alive to the possibilities latent in being and hence one is entirely active.

Spiritual passivity is, then, a kind of contemplative attentiveness; more a listening than a seeing, it becomes an active assimilation of the silence of being.

Ordinary seeing is a playing out of one's interests and modes of selective attention. Contemplative listening is a gathering-up, a bringing together of what is otherwise scattered and disjointed.

Spiritual passivity is thus precisely the opposite of a distraught consciousness. Clearing the mind of anticipations, one becomes as a mirror reflecting a sacred harmony of being.

Complacency: the great danger lurking within passivity.

Spiritual passivity is a state of blessed forgetfulness. Suspending temporality, it opens up an entirely new space for being, every moment becoming a fresh discovery of who one most truly is, for what is received in spiritual passivity is the very truth of spirit; silence divine.

One cannot practice the attainment of spiritual passivity by means of some kind of technique or other; nevertheless it is a practice which one must continually re-learn. And yet if it is regarded as a task and not something entirely spontaneous and natural it will surely not be attained. Spiritual passivity is essentially a state to which one is called, rather than something that one attains as an escape from the humdrum affairs of ordinary living. A false or pseudo-passivity prevails whenever one attempts to make of spiritual passivity the way to a special "experience"—a me-centered, prideful satisfaction.

Spiritual passivity is a retrieving of one's nothingness. It becomes love when one hears a call from within it, beckoning one, as it were, to its graceful power.

Divine Love

Deus caritas est.

Spiritual passivity, contemplation, becomes a loving state of being when it is filled with a radiant power which, desiring nothing, encompasses everything.

Divine love is indiscriminate insofar as it is without objects of its own. It is not, then, a "giving" or a "receiving"; it is not a *relationship* between two or more separate beings; divine love is rather a grace-bestowing presence in which the tranquil, not the overheated, soul finds itself to be at home.

There is a wondrous beauty in this love, a compelling beauty which draws one freely yet irresistibly to its overpowering splendor.

Divine love vanishes for us the moment we let our desires come forth. Divine love, however, is not a call for submission—for this still implies "twoness"; it is, though, a demand for self-surrender, a taking leave of those needs which bind and distort one. Releasing oneself from the little "I," one attains the marvelous strength which accompanies fulfillment.

Divine love, then, is not that of a personal being who loves, but a state of being realized in human consciousness wherein all existence is taken-up and is transfigured and transformed.

Divine love—let us here call it divine goodness—radically "transvaluates" all one's previous values in the light of its radiant power, rendering them, in comparison to itself, as nothing.

No thing could possibly have intrinsic worth if existing apart from this power. Every thing becomes of value when abiding in togetherness with it.

Divine love cannot be willed: one can only strive to remove the impediments to its realization, and then to conduct oneself consistently within its power.

And the self transformed by this love acquires an altogether new and different kind of knowing, an "unknowing knowing," truth become wisdom.

Wisdom

Wisdom is peace and blessedness.

Sophia: but wisdom is neither of woman nor of man.

Wisdom, which is founded on spiritual knowing or "unknowing knowing," rests epistemically on the truth of *omnis determinatio est negatio*; that nothing positive can rightly be asserted about divine reality without at the same time allowing the possibility of its opposite. In the last analysis, then, only a *via negativa* which disallows all attribution is appropriate for the finite mind anxious to know what is inherently unknowable to it. Wisdom is the living, full realization of the impossibility of comprehending the divine in the terms and by the means of our ordinary noetic experience. "Had I a God whom I could understand, I would no longer hold him for God."

Wisdom, then, is a kind of value-play which is made possible by the space opened up by the radical incommesurability between divine reality and our memory-laden constructed worlds. It does not involve knowing about something or other in a special way; it has nothing to do with the "occult"; rather it is an enduring act of recognition—a style of value-seeing that apprehends things and affairs in their proper place. Wisdom, in short, does not deliver knowledge; it tells us what is worth knowing—and especially not-knowing.

There is an innocence in wisdom that often appears childlike but is, in fact, precisely the opposite of naïveté. Setting aside worldly sophistication, one is enabled to see with wonderment and joy the spirit that is everywhere to be seen.

The simplicity of the wise, then, is not the mere opposite of complexity, but is an entirely different qualitative state of being—one which finds its deepest satisfaction in not wanting this or that.

Wisdom is an on-going process of awakening—and it is as well an active detachment from all that is transitory.

Wisdom is a state of acceptance; not as a callous disregard for the evils inflicted upon, and the misery endured by, so many human lives, but as a loving affirmation of that which alone bestows meaning on being.

Part 2

Tales and Plays

The Church

All things perish. Everywhere existence is immersed in the transitory. The chorus of history, and you and me, incessantly affirm this indubitable truth: all things living will die. The impermanent is everywhere stamped on existence.

No one knows why the church continues to exist. Many centuries ago the master builders and masons, who were extremely able and clever men, buried the secret of their art somewhere deep within the delicate vaultings, the slender arches, the graceful columns and buttresses, or, perhaps, even in the very foundations of the church. According to all the known principles of construction, according to all the rules which set forth the acceptable distribution of weight, the balance between stress and strain, according to all the laws of the science of engineering, this sublime church has no reason for existing. It ought to have crumbled to earth, returned to dust, many years ago. Still it remains in the little town of Ulmin, retaining even until today its beauty and its mystery.

The church was a prayer built of stone and wood. Its outward, aspiring rigidity revealed at once that something complex, something restless and unstable was occurring within it. It reflected, and seemed to contain, a great need, as one who is unfulfilled. It gave the impression that all the forces, powers, and possibilities of life were somehow held within and were centered upon it. One realized that there was something here that one could not grasp, something which defied explanation. The church had a subjective character to it which was closed, like all forms of inward life, to an objective gaze.

Scholars, architects, engineers, all of us, visited the church regularly, seeking to discover its secret. There were some who thought that the mystery of the church's construction could be solved by questioning the local townspeople. Ulmin is a very quiet provincial town lying in a low valley surrounded by luxuriant hills. It is known and celebrated for the excellence of its craft-work. The townspeople love their church very much and just slightly object to the many visitors who come here and always ask the same questions. How are they to know the answers? They are only craftsmen of fine furniture and carvings. Many centuries is a long time for a secret of construction as mysterious as this to be handed down and kept alive.

Every year the learned journals carry articles about the church. How many have I read! A brilliant scholar claims to have solved its mystery only to have another scholar refute his claims. The church remains untouched. There are simply no engineering principles by which the church's construction can be understood. Recently, after a period of sustained controversy, one of my colleagues, a professor in France, actually suggested that part of the church should be dismantled; then the structure would be visible and anyone knowledgeable could solve the mystery with his unaided eye. My colleague could with but difficulty understand why so many people wrote to him and expressed their dislike, indeed, almost hatred of him. After all, he only suggested that part of the church should be torn down.

One day, however, the church itself, as though answering his appeal, actually parted with one of its members. How amazed we were to learn that part of the roofing had given way and had fallen in a small heap, almost in the very center of the church! Hundreds of us descended upon Ulmin.

We drew new plans, made new measurements, propounded new theories, refuted others, and convinced no one of the validity of our own. Nothing important at all was revealed from a close study of the now open portion of the roof. The church's construction, I fear, will forever be a closed secret.

The church was crowded, as it was now every day, with visitors who came to study and to witness its mystery. Some were praying in front of the delicately carved wooden altar; others were simply strolling about, speaking softly to one another. Suddenly there was chaos. People were screaming and pushing to make their way to the back of the church. Another part of the church had collapsed. A column had crumbled almost directly in front of those who were praying. There was a great cloud of dust; terrified, everyone fled the building. By the time I had gathered myself together and realized my extraordinary opportunity, the authorities had arrived and forbade anyone, except themselves, to re-enter the church. If only I could have been there with them. I could have seen at once why the church remained standing.

A short time later, the doors of the church opened and the authorities entered the square. The bishop was helped on to a small platform that had been hastily assembled and addressed the silent crowd. They pressed forward to hear him. No one wanted to miss what he had to say. In a loud tremulous voice he commanded "Kneel and pray!" The crowd was uncertain and hesitated, but seeing the bishop stand there with his intimidating presence, they were reassured and did as he ordered. After several moments the bishop in a triumphant voice proclaimed: "A miracle has occurred. A column has collapsed—and the debris cannot, by any human power, be removed."

The crowd was stunned, but then everyone rushed in every direction shouting "Miracle! Miracle!" They ran throughout the town, but there were few to tell it to for almost everyone, natives and visitors alike, had already gathered in the square by the time the bishop gave his remarkable report. The news of course spread throughout

the land and again within days every available mode of
transportation to Ulmin was in service. The town once again
had to open wide its gates to accommodate new visitors.
Here was a miracle that anyone could witness for themselves.

I still hoped to be the first to re-enter the church and
spent the remaining hours of the afternoon avoiding the
crowds, deciding how I might accomplish this end. I waited
until it was dark and approached the church. A large crowd
was still standing in the square, but with an air of authority
I went directly to the main door of the church. Much to my
surprise I found it was unlocked and immediately I went
inside, apparently unnoticed, for who would expect that a
single person might enter the church in the presence of such
a large crowd? The church was empty and silent. As I
approached the debris, though, I noticed someone was sitting
nearby; no doubt the night watchman who had dozed off. I
decided not to awaken him. At the first touch of the debris, I
knew the bishop's words were true. The debris could not be
moved. It was as concentrated gravity.

The light from the watchman's lantern threw long pale
rays up and through the space which separated the base of
the collapsed column from the upper area which it previ-
ously supported. I knew the precise distribution of forces
within the structure of the church and saw at once that
without the support of this fallen column, the whole upper
portion, if not itself falling altogether, should at least disclose
a definite shift of weight. From my position, however, I could
discern no change whatsoever in the upper portion.
Apparently it was unaffected by the loss of the supporting
column. I returned to my quarters and carefully restudied
my drawings and calculations

I have now determined that within a month's time the
entire north wall of the church will collapse. It must happen.
Shall I report this to the authorities? Someone might be
injured when the wall collapses: indeed many might be
killed. Perhaps precautionary measures can be taken to

support the church. New and stronger columns could be added. The beautiful stained-glass windows could be preserved. But if I tell the authorities, and they believe me, and if adequate measures are taken, then my theory, my prediction, can never either be proved or disproved. Nevertheless, it is too great a responsibility.

The bishop was a tall, slender man and possessed a sincere dignity in his bearing. He gave me the feeling that he was at once amused and worried about my prediction. He would think about it and would see me again the next day. The bishop also told me that the church would remain closed for an indefinite time. He wanted things to settle down a bit. After all, he was responsible here for the correct interpretation and handling of these miracles. And they must be kept alive properly.

I returned the next day. The bishop seemed pleased with himself. Naturally he could not consider adding new supports to the church, for if he listened to every engineer who came along, the church would have been dismantled and rebuilt at least a hundred times over. He would, however, make certain that everyone remained some distance from it. Also, he suggested that I tell no one of my prediction. It might cause a great deal of trouble—the townspeople were very nervous and excitable these days—and if the wall did not collapse, which was indeed likely, then I would be in an embarrassing position with my colleagues.

Three weeks later the north wall of the church collapsed. Immediately I rushed to the scene. My calculation was right! The north wall had collapsed! Terror and wonder again spread throughout Ulmin. The authorities would proclaim another miracle. A wall of the church had collapsed and the debris could not be removed. I left the town square, feeling proud and yet confused and saddened. I followed a path up one of the hills surrounding Ulmin and there, in a small nestle of rocks, I sat down and looked over the valley. The sun was just setting behind the hill and long shadows were cast into the town. I saw the church and the remaining stain-glassed windows illuminated by the reflection of the setting sun. It was beautiful.

Within less than an hour the remaining walls, the columns, and roof crashed to the earth. The entire church was as though demolished. The materials all seemed to have returned to their original forms. The debris and rubble were scattered everywhere, as though willing to move only after everything was destroyed.

Innocence

None of the three men would admit that he was guilty of the crime that one of them had committed and which inadvertently saved the other two, as well as himself, from legally owing large sums of money. One of them had to be punished. The three men were highly trusted executives in a bank. Each had borrowed money from the bank, the only security on their loans being personal notes which were kept in a locked safe. The three of them, together with the president of the bank, were the only ones who had access to the safe, which was seldom opened. One afternoon the president opened the safe to place something in it and discovered, with no little surprise and indignation, a heap of ashes. The notes and other papers had been completely burned.

Immediately the president called the police and ordered his three executives to come into his office. Confronted, each proclaimed his own innocence. Who could commit such a crime? The police arrived, recorded all the details, took fingerprints, and informed the president that they could not find any significant clues. The ashes were at least a month old; there was no sign as to how the fire was started; a solution seemed hopeless. The chief of police, a friend of the president, was then called and upon arrival agreed that it looked like an insolvable crime and stated that if the president was convinced that one of the executives had committed the

19

crime then it was up to him to accuse one of them or indeed all three of them if he thought they were in collusion. He also told him that he doubted if he could get an indictment only on the circumstantial evidence that each of them had access to the safe and could have benefited greatly from the crime. The president was then left alone with the three executives. Everyone was silent and embarrassed.

Soon, however, the air was filled with loud proclamations of innocence. Each executive forcibly denied committing the crime. The president told them, then, that they would all remain here until the matter was resolved. They were to call their families and explain that there was an emergency at the bank and that they might have to remain here for some time.

The location of the safe was such that any one of them could open it, anytime of the day, without anyone else being aware of it. The other papers which were destroyed, though valuable, were replaceable and their destruction would benefit no one. Each of the executives informed the president of his financial status. The president was surprised to learn that they were all heavily in debt, but no case was desperate. They each stated that they had used the monies they had borrowed for personal investments which turned out badly. As to other aspects of their private lives, the president refrained from asking. Several hours passed and nothing was accomplished. Each understood, however, the terrible situation which they, and the president, had been forced into.

The president decided he would leave the three executives alone with each other. He informed them that it was up to them to discover which of them was guilty of the crime. If they failed, he would be forced to reconsider all of their positions in the bank. He would wait for them in another room.

Who committed the crime? Was the guilty one actually a hero to the others, having absolved them legally of their large debts, or was he wholly despicable, having brought them to this position of possible disgrace? Who among them had betrayed the president's trust. After much argument, with nothing further being resolved, they became silent, and, for the first time, thoughtful. What will happen now to me, to my family? Soon the silence was intolerable; but who now would be the first to speak. Many minutes passed. No one would break the silence. It was as if they had a tacit agreement that the first one to speak would be the guilty one. He would be the one unable to endure his own conscience. The silence weighed as in a graveyard. It was unbearable. Finally, one of them arose, crossed to the middle of the room, and said to the others: "I am not guilty." The tension was broken, and again they began arguing and lamenting their fate. They accused each other. " You would have benefited from this more than I. You..." It was ugly and degrading. They again fell silent, and were ashamed. They had always been close in their working relationships and socially as well. They was no competition between them as such, for the bank was organized in such a way that each had autonomy in his respective sphere. Their wives were also friends, and they met often in each other's homes.

During this silence, each again asked the question to himself "Who is guilty?" Suddenly one of them realized that being himself innocent, instead of trying to find out out which of the other two was guilty, he should try to seek the other one who is innocent. How to enter into the conscience of another? How to find the other one innocent of the crime? He studied the other two men carefully, and imagined each of them to be innocent. They proved themselves equally well. Either of them could be innocent. He tried again, and again. Suddenly he caught the eye of the man to his left, and he knew! He was also innocent. He, too, was trying to determine who was innocent. They embraced each other almost with tears. The third remained seated. They looked at him with horror. He arose, picked up the phone, and called the president.

The Director

He had inherited great wealth, and was gifted also with a refined sensibility and a keen intelligence. Women sought his company, as he was, by choice, indifferent to them, and men asked his advice, as he was knowledgeable about many things. He could converse with authority on literature and music, political theory and art—and especially the art of the theatre. He had a peculiar passion for the theatre. Whenever he thought back upon his childhood, it was always the make-believe, fantasy side of growing-up that he remembered and loved.

Imagination—reconstructing the world in terms of the possibilities that it suggested: this was the supreme human achievement. He drew no distinction between imagination and fantasy, and hence his love for the theatre. Here one could enter a new world, a world suggested by actuality but never realized there; a world of men, women and things, freely juxtaposed, freely interchanged, the entire action of which was subject to human direction and control. Neither destiny nor necessity were part of the theatre for him. People could be represented as living forever, they could defy gravity, they could become utterly wicked or good, entirely happy or completely miserable—even simple. Everything could be cast into the terms which one chose, and become credible.

22

He lived in a large villa by the sea, alone expect for his servants and the many acquaintances that came so often to visit him. He traveled a great deal to the cities, however, keeping himself informed of the newest developments in politics and the most recent movements in the arts. Although he was seldom elated and seldom depressed, he enjoyed life immensely. He lived an ordered, indeed a tranquil life. When at home in his villa by the sea, he spent most of his time in his study, much of his library consisted of works of and about the theatre.

He was in his study when he had the idea (why had he never thought of it before!)—yes, certainly, he would engage a theatrical group to live and perform here in his own villa and solely for his pleasure and the entertainment of his friends. A magnificent idea!

At first he was content only to watch the actors and actresses rehearse their parts and to observe the many activities involved in arranging the sets, building the platforms, painting the scenery, selecting the costumes. The little auditorium that he had built was indeed filled with the most fascinating activity. He enjoyed the preparations greatly; but finally he inquired of the director when the first performance could be held. But the rehearsals and the arrangements would always take just another week or so. The troupe enjoyed living in this wonderful villa, taking carefree walks in the gardens and by the sea, dining in the old paneled hall, being waited upon and catered to. Perhaps their patron would not like the play or perhaps having once seen them perform he would change his mind and return to his study.

At last the play was ready to be performed. He invited many friends and acquaintances and prepared for a gala occasion. He attended personally to sending the invitations, to selecting the menus, to all the little details necessary for making a splendid evening.

The play was tolerably performed. It was about a young woman and a young man who, due to a series of extraordinary circumstances, found themselves alone in a garden.

They were innocent of worldly concerns and demands. Delicious fruits and cool waters were available to them. The play related the way in which this charming pair discovered one another physically and morally, and how they suffered the consequences of their discovery.

He enjoyed himself thoroughly. This was a delightful world of light and dark: everything was presented in bold contrasts, male and female, innocence and corruption, joy and despair. His guests too seemed to enjoy the evening.

He invited the troupe to take a vacation for a week; they could do whatever they might want to do. He, however, would have a busy week. He remained in his study the whole time, except of course for meals and the rest, thinking, planning, reliving the play in his mind. At the end of the week he announced that instead of a new play the same one that had been performed was to be rehearsed and performed again.

In the weeks that followed, the patron became more then ever involved in the work of the troupe. He could no longer just sit in the auditorium and watch what was happening. He would say a word or two to the director; this part should be spoken a bit softer, this movement was a bit abrupt, that light could be better focused. The director complied as best he could. Each day the patron spent more time with the troupe. He neglected everything else. He demanded more and more from the actors; all the sets had to be rebuilt; all the costumes re-designed. He assumed, in fact, all the responsibilities of the director.

He was never satisfied. The play was still imperfect. So many aspects of the meeting between the young woman and the young man could be improved upon. Weeks and even months passed. He no longer received guests and when his friends inquired about the troupe and when the next performance might be held, he was evasive, and soon didn't bother to answer their inquiries at all.

The players at times found the constant rehearsals and incessant changes somewhat tedious, but living here in the manner provided for was still very much to their taste, and he continually urged them on. He became one of them. And the troupe never did perform another play. They simply rehearsed the garden scene.

The End

Characters

Leader (fortyish white man)

1st Lieutenant (fortyish white woman)

2nd Lieutenant (fiftyish white man)

3rd Lieutenant (thirtyish white man)

Group

Member (twentyish black woman)

Member (thirtyish white man)

Member (teenage white girl)

Member (twentyish black man)

Member (sixtyish white woman)

Member

Member

Member

Member

Setting, throughout the play, is outdoors; a clearing in a wooded area. It is summertime (or anytime in a naturally warm climate); the characters are lightly clothed. All the characters wear masks: the nine members of the group in white and black (some all-black, some all-white, others one-quarter, two-quarters, and three-quarters white—or black); the lieutenants wear red and white masks, somewhat more elaborate, each slightly, but distinguishably, different from the others; the leader wears a multicolored mask.

Scene 1

> *[The nine members of the group are gathered informally in a semi-circle around a slightly raised platform. Standing on the platform is the leader, in a rather rigid, triumphant posture. At the bottom of the platform, standing as if they were guards, are the leader's three lieutenants. The scene opens with the chanting of the group]*

Group
> He is the way
> And the life
> And the glory.
> He is the truth
> And the love
> And the power.
> Saved by him
> I am redeemed.
> Loved by him
> I am fulfilled
> Now
> And forevermore
> In the new life
> That will come
> With the End.

Leader
> Will you live with me?

Group
  Yes!

Leader
  Will you die for me?

Group
  Yes, O yes!

Leader
  Who are you?

Group
  Nothing.

Leader
  Who am I?

Group
  Everything.

Leader
  Listen carefully then. It has been said that I exploit you;
  that you are no better-off now than when I lifted you out of
  the sewer and the gutter, the whorehouse and the slaugh-
  terhouse; it has been said that I have stolen your minds
  and your souls and that I have abused your bodies. But we
  know differently: for now you have my love, and although
  my ways may sometimes seem strange, you are assured
  that I care for you, that you do belong to this our family.

Group
  Yes, O yes!
  We are nothing: you are everything. And therefore with
  you we become something

Leader
  When some of you first met me you were surprised to see
  how ordinary I appeared. You expected to see with only
  your little eyes, some measure of greatness—a tall, strong,
  commanding sort of person—while what you saw was just
  what you might see on any busy city street: an accountant,

perhaps a school teacher, the assistant head of a small government office, or the branch manager of your bank. Yes, you wondered, almost aloud (at least I could hear you): "Did I make a stupid mistake? This couldn't be him of whom it is said—'He is the way'." But you quickly learned that your little eyes see nothing worthy of being seen; that to see me you need what only I myself can give you, the loving eyes of faith. And now you see me as I am.

Group

And we rejoice!

Leader

And now you know yourselves.

Group

And we no longer lament.

Leader

Come forward then, those of you that will, and tell—but briefly—your story.

[Twentyish black female member of the Group comes forward]

Member

Some would say that I just needed someone, anyone, to protect me, to look after me, to care for me: and O yes, they were right. I needed someone badly. I'd been raped, beaten, then cast aside, like putrid leftovers from an uneatable meal. I tell you it is pure shit out there. I hate the bastards, the motherfuckers, the dudes, the bosses, the fine ladies—ladies my ass! Here we are one color, or no color; anyway it doesn't matter. I work hard here; but it feels good. I still can't believe it! I work in the kitchen, chopping vegetables and cleaning up, washing dishes and setting tables sometime too. It's crazy. I love it. Why just yesterday I actually sang a song!

[Thirtyish white male member of group comes forward]

Member

Unlike with the others here, at first he needed me more
than I needed him; at least I thought so. For I had everything. I was a teacher teaching English—actually early
American literature was my field—and I was good at it,
and at other things too. Well, it is true that my wife left
me, claimed that I ignored her; took the three kids with
her to Ohio; but I had plenty of lady friends. And I was
writing a book on Emerson—that pompous ass. But I
wanted to start all over again. To begin once more. I
wanted to shed my past, like a snake ridding itself of its
skin; I wanted to forget; to be as one who is just beginning,
with infinite possibilities.

*[Teenage white female member of group comes
forward]*

Member

Drugs was my thing. The needle, the joint, the pill—
anything. I could get off for days. No I didn't have to steal
or sell myself to get the stuff. My father is a doctor. Not
that he gave me the stuff; but he did give me the money,
my god he's got enough of it, and he must have known
what I did with it. Hell, how else do you spend a thousand
or more a week and have nothing to show for it? Not even
a car!

*[Twentyish black male member of group comes
forward]*

Member

Dignity! That one word sums it all up for me. I tried to
make a revolution. Revolution!—what a joke. How do you
get people to revolt when they can't even see what the
problem is? And those that did? Christ, they were no better
off than the blind. They only wanted power. They only
wanted all the crap the others had. No. The political ain't
where it's at. Here, with the spiritual, there is dignity.

*[Sixtyish white female member of group comes
forward]*

Member

Well there is so much to say, and yet so little. I was a Zen
Buddhist before I met him. I was also active, at one time,
with the Ramakrishna-Vivekenanda Order in New York;
but they became too Christian for me; what with their
sermons and charities and everything. He, on the other
hand, is just right. Why you've heard his voice. How can
anyone doubt that he has the spirit—that he is the spirit?
Oh, it's so thrilling! Here we are, like the early disciples,
making history!

Leader

Let us extend our hands.

> *[Leader stretches hands toward lieutenants; they raise
> their arms upward; members of the group stretch
> theirs toward the lieutenants]*

Leader, Lieutenants, Group

Belonging together
We are united
And will sacrifice anything
Or anyone
For the sake of this
Our family.

Group

O merciful one!
You are the way.
We have nothing to give you
But you take it and multiply it
And nothing becomes
Something wonderful.
Please, O please, make love to us now.
Let us receive you.
Let us feel that which throws open the night
Into blazing light
Rising, expanding, exploding.

> *[Each member of group, by him / herself, acts out ritu-
> alized, ecstatic love-making, as though with leader,
> until exhausted, they depart.*

*Leader and Lieutenants in same positions but
are now relaxed.]*

1st Lieutenant

Among your trusted ones, I, your dearest disciple, also
proclaim: I love you, but not as they do, the filthy scum,
looking always toward their own satisfaction, their little
orgasms which they confound with true ecstasy. I love you
purely, asking nothing in return, asking only that you find
me worthy enough to accept my love.

2nd Lieutenant [To himself]

And I too am trusted by him. Indeed, he doesn't really
have a choice; for I know so much more than the others. I
know about the dollars, the francs, the pounds, the yen,
the marks; I should know about it—having managed the
whole thing. O yes, we collect well, especially for what we
give and pay back in return. It has been rumored, I have
heard it myself, that we are vastly wealthy. Well if you call
seventy-five million a lot of money, then indeed that is
what we are. Yes, the coins add up; and the legacies too.
The stuff the riffraff bring in when they first join us isn't
worth keeping records for; but there are a few nice big
ones. Delicious! Some of the biddies had so much they
didn't even know how much they had. But we took it all—
and I keep the records. And the coins the riff-raff bring in
do add up, as I say. A coin here, a coin there, and soon
there are thousands of dollars a day. My first, and only, job
after I finished school was with a bank. O yes, I know the
business well. I know what it means to borrow and lend.
Ah, the poor slobs who really needed the money. We only
gave to those who already had it. We helped them to accu-
mulate more. We got our share. Miserable business: it was
all to no purpose.

3rd Lieutenant

I am strong
And will always protect you.

No one would dare harm you
With me here.
For I'd tear out their eyes
Bust their balls
Rip their lungs and livers
And throw their kidneys
To the dogs.
I'm the muscle here
And I love my work.
Everyone is afraid of me
Even you sometimes
When I pretend to be angry
So that you
Will pay attention to me.

Lieutenants [Together]
Who can deny it?
The world
Is coming to the End
And we, through you, will be saved.
The End will be spectacular.
As you have said
There will be a bang
A deafening roar
A light so strong
Nothing else will be seen.
The whole galaxy will explode
Everything will be
Annihilated to make room
For the void.
Nothing can prevent it
The End will come
And soon.
But we will be saved.
We have been selected
To build a new world
To be governed by you

To be nurtured by the love
Which binds us
Together
As a family.
It will be magnificent!
  [Lieutenants leave, leader stands alone, in same posi-
  tion, on the platform]

Leader
  They do love me
  And they should
  For in my innermost being
  I know—I feel—with certainty
  That I am special
  Someone with a mission
  With the truth
  With the way.
  Everything that has happened—wars and revolutions; rela-
  tions with friends and family; everyday little things; where
  I have lived, when I would go to work—seems to have
  conspired to protect and direct me, to make possible this my
  mission to lead others to the End. In some mysterious way
  my life has been under a divine guidance. I know it. I feel it.
  Yes, I am someone special, someone very special indeed.
      But whence derives this extraordinary power of
  mine? That is easy! It comes from being without an ego.
  Oh you laugh. You think I am joking. But you misunder-
  stand. When I use the term 'I'—unlike you—I don't mean
  this thing you see in front of you—this body which weighs
  170 pounds and is 5 feet 10 inches tall and which suppos-
  edly houses a rational mind and irrational appetites; no,
  when I use the term 'I'—unlike you—I mean reality itself.
  Yes, a divine reality, which knows no difference between
  itself and my real self. O glorious power! O life divine!

Group [From afar]
  He is the way
  And the truth

And the glory
He is the power
Which sustains our life.

Scene 2

[Three lieutenants sitting on the platform, relaxed, alone]

1st Lieutenant

You mustn't pay attention to this nonsense we hear—especially in the papers—that he is corrupt, a stealer of souls; that his followers are made mindless in order that he may control them.

2nd Lieutenant

Yes, but were we wise we would watch out for ourselves too. We would have a contingency plan; something to fall back upon should the worse happen.

3rd Lieutenant [to 2nd]

Nothing will happen so long as I am here.

2nd Lieutenant [to 3rd]

What will you do against rifles and tanks; the police, the army. You can't frighten them with your muscles, you idiot.

3rd Lieutenant [to 2nd]

Watch your language, comrade, or you'll be the first to see what I can do.

1st Lieutenant

This is crazy; this contentiousness is madness. It is obvious that we must always stick together, but instead, while the plotting goes on, we bicker among ourselves. If, as I have always said, we remain true to our principles, if we adhere closely to our beliefs, if we ourselves are as we should be—nothing can threaten us, no one can rightfully accuse us of anything.

2nd Lieutenant
And what about the stash?

1st and 2nd Lieutenants [together]
The what?

2nd Lieutenant
The stash. The cash. The treasure. I've done my best to
hide it—in the modern way—in thirty different compa-
nies, with interlocking directorates, in countless accounts,
each borrowing from, and lending to, the other. The stuff
is at least (but only) three months away from any gang of
auditors. I suppose the only army we really need fear is
that of the number-crunchers, the pencil-pushers, the
punch-key pressers; in short the accountants with their
mindless computers. *[Aside]* Needless to say we never paid
taxes on the stuff.

3rd Lieutenant
I still don't know what he is talking about.

1st Lieutenant [to 3rd]
Perhaps it is best you don't try to understand.

3rd Lieutenant [to 2nd]
OK, smart ass: enough of this mumbo-jumbo. I don't know
what you are talking about and I don't care. The real questions are: Who is the enemy? And how do we get to him?

2nd Lieutenant
The enemy, my friend, is pervasive. Whoever out there is a
potential follower is probably now our enemy as well. Our
only friend is indifference. Lots of people, all kinds of people,
feel threatened by us; the believers (the miserable hypo-
crites) in other supposed ways; the parents (helpless fail-
ures) of what are now our children; the intellectuals (the
ineffectual fools) who are too self-centered to really care
about anything; not to mention industrialists, journalists,
and lawyers—the parasites. Our only friends are perhaps
the farmers; they don't concern themselves about us, not
having heard about us—but even that might not be so.

1st Lieutenant

That sounds like a lot of enemies and very few friends.

2nd Lieutenant

It is, my friend, believe me, it is. And there is no way that I know of to get at them, as Muscles here would put it. The only thing we can do is to be certain that we don't break any of their criminal laws. We'll have to be protected by that for which we have total contempt.

[Lieutenants wander off; leader enters and casually walks about]

Leader

It is true, as the newspapers say; once I was an automobile salesman. I sold Buicks. New ones, though, not used ones. For thirteen years I sold new Buicks. I never got married. No, it has nothing to do with what the newspapers have been hinting about. They wouldn't dare say it outright. No, it is not that I prefer men or boys to women or girls. I loved many a woman—and, Oh yes, a few men and boys too. But one had only to look around to see that marriage was a prison. One day I realized—yes, it came to me quite suddenly—that I was, as I've said before, someone very special. For one thing I could sell a Buick to almost anyone. I could charm a customer so that he felt obliged to buy from me and was even apologetic if something turned out wrong with his car. And of course there was something more. A gut feeling of not really being a part of this buying and selling, this pushing and shoving, laughing and crying that we call our lives. I realized that I had a mission; that I was born to lead. I realized that I could see the coming of the End. And so I did gather in my followers. Losers mostly; young people, but also quite a few older ones too. They were desperate seekers all right; and their only hope lay in the awareness of their despair. They could be saved. And I have saved them. Yes, they paid a price, I suppose—but don't we all?

One thing I didn't expect, though, was the fury of the others. This is not some wild hysterical mob arrayed against me now, but a coalition of so-called respectable citizens. They hate me with the same intensity as my followers love me. But I don't understand this sort of thing. They should be grateful to me. I did, to be sure, dabble in a little politics—which I probably shouldn't have done—for that is an enemy-making business if there ever was one; but usually there the enemy, the opponent, doesn't seek utterly to destroy one.

I am afraid. I must admit it. We could go abroad, I suppose. But whoever would have us would only want to use us for their own purposes. But, if I am to be destroyed here, I would be destroyed as well elsewhere.

[1st Lieutenant rushes in]

1st Lieutenant
Is it true? If it is, it will surely be the end of us!

Leader
What are you babbling about?

1st Lieutenant
That he has left. Run away!

Leader
No one leaves us—ever.

1st Lieutenant
It can't be true! He told me himself about the treasure. He said it would take an army of accountants at least three months to find it. He would never leave.

Leader
I'll be god-damned!

1st Lieutenant
Oh, you mustn't say that!

Leader
Oh, shut up! Ah, what's this?
[3rd lieutenant drags in 2nd lieutenant, the runaway]

3rd Lieutenant

Look who I found in the woods, with a suitcase full of record books and all of his clothes. Seems he was planning to take a little trip—if he wasn't already on his way.

2nd Lieutenant

Let me explain.

1st Lieutenant

Kill him! Kill him!

Leader

We must first know what he knows. Sometimes you are even dumber than I thought you were.

1st Lieutenant [aside]

What! He thinks I'm stupid?

2nd Lieutenant

You are mistaken in thinking I would betray you. Yes, I was leaving. I've had enough. I suddenly realized that with the accountants coming after me, it is just like it was in the bank. I've had enough of that! You'll easily find someone to replace me. After all I wasn't very important to your spiritual business, only to your financial stuff—and there are plenty of my kind around. And in truth, as you know, I was never altogether convinced of this whole show. I realize that as well as having helped yourself you have helped a lot of people, but I think we've all gotten carried away by this obsession with the End. We've forgotten what it means to be alive. No, I would never betray you. But, yes, I was leaving.

Leader

And the suitcase of records?

2nd Lieutenant

For protection. They show clearly enough where everything is.

Leader

Protection against whom?

2nd Lieutenant
  Them. You. Anyone.

Leader
  You know what we must do now.

2nd Lieutenant
  You don't have to do anything. You are the law here. You
  are not subject to it. You can do whatever you want to do.
  You will do whatever you wish to do.

Leader [to 1st lieutenant]
  Put the records in a safe place.

Leader [to 3rd lieutenant]
  Take him back into the woods—and bury him alive!
    *[3rd lieutenant drags out 2nd lieutenant, who, strug-
    gling, cries out]*

2nd Lieutenant
  You are breaking their laws now!
    [Group enters]

Group
  There is talk that there is trouble
  Both within and without.

1st Lieutenant [gleefully]
  He will be buried alive!
  He will be buried alive!

Group
  What? Who? Why?

Leader
  I have so commanded.
    [Member of the group steps forward]

Member
  Tell us, please, what is happening here.

Group
  Yes, tell us please.

Leader

A terrible crime has been committed. We were almost betrayed, and by one whom I trusted dearly. But no one can betray us, can leave us, and live. That was your commitment: there is no life without me.

[Moans and murmurs from the group. Another member of the group steps forward.]

Member

I hear that they are coming soon to destroy us, to try to break up this our family. I hear that they are very strong and that they can indeed destroy us.

Leader

That is possible. But there is nothing to fear. The worst that could happen would be that we must die.

Group

We must live. Not die. We must live.

Leader

Dying is no sacrifice
When it is for me.
Listen carefully.
Be not afraid.
If we must die
Then what we have started here
We will complete there.
We shall never be separated
For to be separate is to die
Their kind of death.

Group

But what about the End?

Leader

The End will come whether we are here physically or there spiritually. In any event you will be saved.

Group
  O yes
  He is the way
  And the truth
  And the glory
  He is the power
  That sustains our life.

Entre scene

> *[The leader is having a nightmare. Lights are focused in turn on individual disembodied masks from which voices are heard. Lights flash intermittently: a continual eerie groan is heard throughout.]*

Voice of 2nd Lieutenant
  You are the law! You are the law!

Voice of 1st Lieutenant
  I love you. I hate you. As no one else does.

Voice of Group
  We want to live; we want to live!

Voice of Member of Group
  You are not the way.

Voice of 2nd Lieutenant
  Murderer! Charlatan! Murderer!

Leader's Voice
  Let me go.
  I hate them
  I am getting old.
  I hate you.
  English roses
  Sandpipers on the beach
  The waves rolling and thundering

Scene 3

*[Leader is sitting alone. From his appearance—
unshaven and unkempt—it is evident that a considerable period of time has elapsed.]*

Leader

Am I the way? Nothing is changing in this mad world. It
doesn't seem to be coming any closer to an end. At least not
the end I saw for it. Oh, it might blow itself to pieces. But
that wouldn't matter much. Everyone has expected that for
a long time. I saw something cosmic; a terrible annihilation, not a catastrophe made by men. I saw a severe judg-
ment: one that would allow for my real first coming.

Maybe this business with the End is only a silly obsession. Maybe it was only a gimmick to impress the ignorant.
Or am I the one who is ignorant? Anyway this having to
kill some of my followers and provide for others is ridicu-
lous. I am their leader; but ought I to be their leader any
longer? I can't trust anyone. It's boring. And these terrible
dreams. After all this time, hearing him scream.

Oh, how can I be a liberator if I am not myself fully
liberated? If I need followers then surely I am unfit to lead.
A vagabond, a wanderer....I must now possess myself and
renounce everything else. I too must start all over again.

*[Enter two members of the group: the young black
woman and the thirtyish white man]*

Black Woman of Group

You seem forlorn
Sitting here alone.
I thought I heard you
Talking to yourself.

White Male Member of Group

You are needed in the kitchen
There is an argument going on
Over whether we should eat
Fish or meat tonight.

Leader
> It doesn't matter
> Why should I care?
> Why does everything always
> Sink to the stomach?
> I'm tired of this trivia
> This settling of arguments
> This dull routine of
> Love-making and talking
> I want to be alone
> I want to examine everything
> Once more.
> Go, leave me alone.
>> *[The two members of the group, murmuring to each other, move to another part of the clearing, where they are joined by the other members of the group; the leader remains sitting alone]*

Other Members of Group
> Where is he?
> Did you see him?
> What did he say?

Black Female Member of Group
> He wants to be left alone.

White Male Member of Group
> He doesn't care what we eat.
> It isn't important, he says
> It might not even be important
> If we eat at all.

Other Members of Group
> It is important to us.
> We don't, to be sure, live
> By food alone; but still
> To live we need our food
> And other things too!
>> *[Enter 1st and 3rd Lieutenants]*

Lieutenants
   What is all this yapping about?
   Why are you not doing
   Whatever you are supposed to be doing?

Group
   We are worried
   It seems he no longer cares.
   We are worried
   That we will be abandoned.
   We fear
   That he might leave us
   And that we will become no-ones
   Once more.
      *[Twentyish black woman member of group comes
      forward]*

Member of Group
   I'm terrified; I must admit
   I'm scared of being forsaken
   I can't be now
   What I was before.
   I would be lost, yes really lost
   I wouldn't know which way to go
   Without him.
      [White thirtyish male member of group comes forward]

Member of Group
   I didn't need him
   At first
   He needed me
   But now it is different.
   He is my past as well as my future
   I am bound to him
   For without him
   I have neither a past nor a future
   And surely not a present.
      [Teenage white girl comes forward]

Member of Group
　　I've been off the stuff
　　The needle, the pills
　　Too long now to return
　　To want to return
　　But would I be the way
　　I am now
　　Without him?
　　Could I go back as I now am
　　Or would I go back and
　　Only become what I was?
　　　　[Twentyish black man comes forward]

Member of Group
　　What is loyalty and trust
　　If not a commitment
　　To remain together?
　　This ego-crap is intolerable!

Other Members of Group [together]
　　We are worried
　　He no longer cares
　　We are frightened
　　He will leave us
　　We are anxious
　　He will desert us
　　And that there will be
　　No End.

1st Lieutenant
　　You must be mad
　　Of course he cares.
　　Why else do you think
　　He is driven to such worry
　　If not that he constantly
　　Thinks of you?

3rd Lieutenant
　　That's right.

Group

> But why then does
> He avoid us?
> He never sees us
> We never see him
> Day after day.
> We demand that
> He come forward
> That he talk to us
> Make love to us
> And allay these
> Terrible fears.

1st Lieutenant

> It might be a good idea
> If first I spoke with him.

Group [rather menacingly]

> Go then and speak with him.
> We are very worried.
>> *[Group disperses; 1st lieutenant joins leader]*

1st Lieutenant

> The gang is restless
> They want to see you
> They feel threatened by
> Your absence, by
> —if I may so—
> Your senseless
> Withdrawal.

Leader

> Senseless it very well might be
> For I realize now
> There isn't much sense in all
> This childish play.

1st Lieutenant

> Childish play! But remember
> The End.

Leader

I doubt if it will come.

1st Lieutenant

What! Why that is heretical! It can't be said. It can't be heard. You must put aside these awful doubts and rejoin your faithful followers. The gang is restless, I tell you. You must perform your duty.

Leader

Duty? Am I then to be enslaved by what I myself have created? How can I be the Way when I don't believe any longer that there is an End or that, if there were, I am the one who alone can lead others to it? I can no longer be their leader. And why should I be blamed? But blame me if you will. I don't care. It is all so much foolishness; this playing like we are some primitive tribe with its big chief and little tribesmen. I want to be with some men who struggle to make a living, who laugh, argue, and fight, and with a woman with whom I can really share whatever it is I might have to offer.

1st Lieutenant

But I at least have given you everything. I've kept nothing hidden from you.

Leader

When you are transparent—thinking that makes for intimacy—nothing is seen. I'm tired of your being so available to me that you own nothing of yourself. I'm bored with your familiarity. I want to know once again what it is like to meet a stranger, someone who is mysterious to herself and therefore to me, someone who knows what it means to endure being human.

And so you see. I can't be your leader any longer. I must find out once again what I myself am capable of becoming.

1st Lieutenant
> That is impossible!
> No one can leave
> Or ever return.
> Each of us is
> What we are
> Because of the other
> Because of you.
> It is impossible
> To unmake oneself.
> We can only go forward
> And await now
> The End
>> *[Group enters]*

Group
> Talk to us
> Make love to us
> Show us that you care!

Leader [with ennui]
> None of you understand
> None of you seem capable
> Of understanding.
> Very well then
> You will see.
> Everyone extend hands!
>> *[1st lieutenant stands somewhat aside from leader; group forms a three-quarter circle around them with arms outstretched toward leader. A kind of disintegrating, desultory love-making then proceeds and continues until the leader and 1st lieutenant wander off. Group regathers.]*

Group
> It wasn't the same
> It didn't feel right
> Something was lacking

It was as though, and
For the first time,
He was looking only
Toward his own satisfaction
As if he were using us
Not really caring.
It was just like it was out there
Tedious, disgusting
We must do something.
Without our leader
We are worse off than before.
To give up something bad
And not to have it replaced
By anything
Is intolerable.
We must do something!

Twentyish Black Female Member of Group
I wanted to be free
But this is a worse slavery
Being bound to his needs.

Sixtyish White Female Member of Group
O my. Now I shall have to find another
One such as he was.

Twentyish White Male Member of Group
You saw what happened
To one who tried to leave.

Other Members of Group
We must be bold
We must do the unspeakable.
Let us do it now
While we have the courage
And the resolve.
    [Group rushes off stage]

Leader [from afar]
What! You would have me dead?
O no! Not like this!
   [screams]

   [Group gathers anxiously back in the clearing. 1st lieutenant stands on platform. 3rd lieutenant stands at bottom, as if on guard.]

1st Lieutenant
Will you live with me?

Group
Yes.

1st Lieutenant
Will you die for me?

Group
Yes, O yes!

1st Lieutenant
Who are you?

Group
Nothing.

1st Lieutenant
Who am I?

Group
Everything!

1st Lieutenant
Listen carefully, then...

Francis

On stage are four platforms: nos. 1 and 2 are raised slightly higher than the others. On platform no. 1 various actions will be depicted against a backdrop with changing scenery. On platform no. 2 the town square of Assisi will be continuously represented. On no. 3, which will remain bare, an actor playing Francis and dressed in a Franciscan habit, will remain throughout the performance. On no. 4 a chorus of five monks, also dressed in Franciscan habits, will remain throughout the play.

ACT I

Scene 1

[Francis, in 1207, twenty-five years old (on platform no. 2), is dressed stylishly, moving across the town square of Assisi with a group of drinking companions, singing]

Francis
O once I saw a maiden bare
Who called to me
And—
[Francis falls behind the others and suddenly remains motionless, as if in a trance]

52

Companions
  Francis! Francis! Where are you? What are you thinking
  about? Or whom are you lustfully dreaming about?
  *[Laughter. Francis startled, as if brought back from a
  deep sleep, announces:]*

Francis
  I shall marry the noblest and the most beautiful lady ever
  to be seen.
  *[Companions laugh mockingly, but noticing the
  intense, transfigured expression of Francis, fall silent]*

Chorus
  Francis. Francis.
  Shameless, irresponsible
  A self-appointed leader
  Of drunkards and fools
  A wild spender
  Of his father's money
  On feasts and on girls.
  Francis. Francis.
  You are in love now
  With something nameless
  With someone unseen.

Scene 2

  *[Companions disperse. Francis' costume is so made as
  to allow him to turn around, change and reappear in
  simple clothes. Francis gives alms to beggars who
  enter the town square. Beggars disperse. While this is
  being enacted on no. 2, another actor depicting
  Francis, and similarly dressed in simple clothes, is
  shown on no. 1 in a mountainous area with a small
  cavern. He is with an unidentified companion who
  waits by the outside as Francis enters the cavern and
  is seen silhouetted near the opening, kneeling. With
  agonized voice]*

Francis

O Lord! O dear Lord! Forgive me! You have before you the worst sinner of all. I have wasted my life. My life will always be a waste without You. Loving You, I hate myself. This despicable body! This soul blackened with sin! I am filthy, unworthy of having been born. Oh, what a fool I have been, thinking that sensual pleasure could make me happy. There is no happiness apart from You. This miserable me is nothing—and is no doubt less than nothing to You. O Lord! O dear Lord! Forgive me! Let me serve You. Let me be your fool alone.

Chorus

What anguish, what torment
Does he who aspires to goodness know
When he meets himself
In the raw
Without pretense
In solitude.
Is there any misery deeper
Than that of a soul
Come to see itself
Steeped in sin?
We recognize that sin
In contrast to the purity
Yet remaining in ourselves
To be recovered
By our effort and
His grace.
And so Francis left that cave
On Mount Subasio
Broken, sorrowful
Yet hopeful.

> *[Francis, standing alone on no. 3, facing and addressing the audience]*

Francis

What was I to do? A merchant's son, a clothier. I was willing to go naked; to give everything away for the sake of His love. I was told once by a mysterious voice to return home from where I was and to wait to hear what I must do. I found the answer while visiting a little church, San Damiano, near Assisi. I heard a crucifix speak. Yes, I heard it. It was terrifying. I was alone in the church, which had fallen into disrepair. I was kneeling before the image, absorbed in its mystery, when suddenly the image said to me: "Francis, you must repair my house." I was overwhelmed and I was very naïve; and so I did everything I could to rebuild that and other churches in the area. In fact, much to my regret at that time, I tried to do too much.

Chorus

Francis moved stones
And carried heavy beams.
Francis worked harder
Than any laborer before him.
But it takes money to repair churches
To buy materials
To pay for help from others.
So what did Francis do?
In all innocence, without thinking
He went to his father's clothing store
In his father's absence
And helped himself to the finest goods
And sold them.

Scene 3

[Pietro di Bernardone, Francis' father, on no. 1, enters a wooded area near a small church, shouting]

Father

Where is Francis? Where are my goods? I have given him everything—and he steals from me!
[A group of Bernardone's friends gather with him and together they start a search for Francis. Hearing them, Francis appears before them.]

Friends

Coward! Thief!

[They fling mud and throw stones at him. Bernardone grabs Francis and slaps his face repeatedly, crying out]

Father

You ungrateful scum! You're no better than a miserable beggar. How dare you steal from me!

[Bernardone pulls Francis by the hair and drags him away, shouting]

You will renounce your rights of inheritance. You will not be my heir.

Scene 4

[On no. 2, in the town square a large crowd is gathered. Francis is standing before his father and the local bishop, who had approved of Francis' disinheritance]

Father

Here before your bishop and the witness of our neighbors I demand that you renounce your rights as heir to my estate.

Francis

Gladly. I hereby renounce all rights as heir to your estate. And here take these as well.

[Francis removes all his clothes and flings them on the ground before his startled father]

Francis

And I renounce you Pietro di Bernardone as my father! Here, then, you have everything. My father is He who art in heaven. He alone is my father!

Father

Who are you to renounce me? You, for whatever you are worth, belong to me. You are no longer my heir—but you are still mine to dispose of. You are my flesh and blood. To lose me would be to commit suicide.

Francis

Henceforth I shall be dead to this world. I shall be in the service of my true father. No, I am not yours: we are all only His alone.

[The bishop throws a cloak over Francis and embraces him. Francis then departs, joyously singing]

Francis

Lord! O Lord! With your blessing I am now free!

Chorus

Is there anything more hideous
Than a leper far gone
In his affliction?
Pus pouring out through open sores
Part of his nose and mouth missing
His flesh stinking
His deformed shape rotting
Before your eyes.
Francis, once so fastidious
Francis, in his newfound joy
Came across a leper in the woods
A horrible smelling one in filthy rags
And Francis kissed him
On his oozing sore.

[Francis on no. 3 and the chorus on no. 4 recite simultaneously]

Francis

And then I became a wanderer, suffering gladly for my Lord. But what does it mean to endure humiliations, to be hungry, to be cold, to be regarded as mad? It means nothing when He is with me. Having no house, my home was wherever I found myself to be. I rebuilt churches. I have always loved churches. And I will always be loyal to the Church—even when, as now, it is troubled: priests

living in luxury while the poor starve; lust in the highest
as well as lowest places.

Chorus

And so Francis preached.
He preached to anyone
Who would listen to him.
Simply, directly, he spoke of sin
But more importantly he spoke of love.
And soon he had a following.
O Bernard of Quintavalle
You rich and famous doctor of law
You became his first known disciple.
Having offered Francis hospitality in
Your manor house
You talked with him at length.
Then in the middle of the night
While pretending to sleep
You watched Francis get out of bed
You watched Francis pray fervently
You watched Francis become bathed in light
You saw Francis in ecstasy
Consumed in the radiant energy of love.

Scene 5

[On no. 1, in the library of Bernard's manor house]

Bernard

I have resolved, Francis, to abandon everything and to
follow you. Never before have I felt with such certainty
that this is what I must do. As you can see, I am not
fleeing from hardship, but from abundance. I am said to
be learned and to be very clever at winning arguments.
But truth, I now see—and I see it in you—is not something apart from he who utters it. You must let me be your
disciple. I will follow wherever you lead.

Francis

Let us not be hasty—for there can be no returning to what you are now when once you follow His path. If one is to renounce everything, then indeed nothing remains. You must be certain that this is what is required of you.

Bernard

I am willing to risk everything.

Francis

Before deciding, let us consult the Gospel.

[Francis picks up the book and opens it randomly]

Francis

Here is Matthew (19:21): "If you would be perfect, go, sell what you possess and give to the poor, and you will have treasure in heaven; and come, follow me."

And here is Luke (9:3) "Take nothing for your journey, no staff, nor bag, nor bread, nor money..."

And here is Luke (9:23) again: "if any man would come after me, let him deny himself and take up the cross daily and follow me."

Yes, come Bernard. The Gospel confirms you.

[Simultaneously with scene 6]

Chorus

And Peter of Catania joined them
And a priest Sylvester
And the illiterate countryboy Giles
Who would be one of Francis' favorites
And others like John and Philip the Tall
Sabbastino and Morico
Whom Francis sent on teaching missions
Always two together.
They begged for their food
And when none was received
They fasted
With thanks.
Eight brothers then

Traveled as beggars
Crazy in the Lord.

Scene 6

[On no. 1, Francis is alone in a wooded area]

Francis

What, O Lord, would you have me do now? I see my disciples, your children, reaching across the earth. O Lord! Am
I given to convert the whole world? Why have you chosen
me as their leader? How can I know that it is right for me
to ask another, even in your name, to become nothing and
to follow me? I feel your presence, your spirit, working
within me. But is it truly You or just a figment of my imagination? Is it You or only what I want to be? Help me, O
Lord! Give me strength and confidence so that I may carry
out your will. With You I will convert the whole world.

ACT II

Scene 1

[Francis on no. 3]

Francis

Was it because my father was absent when I was born that
he never understood me? A pilgrim came to our house—
sometime in early 1182, so I was told—and prophesied that
I was to be either among the best or among the worst of
men. I was the worst. And then that name "Francesco,"
"Frenchman," "Francis"—that my father insisted I bear
after he finally returned from a business trip to France,
"Giovanni" I was baptized before his return. A lovely name,
after John the Baptist, chosen by my dear mother. But
Pietro di Bernardone, my father, would hear nothing of it.
"Francesco" it was to be. "Francesco Bernardone," "Francis
of Assisi."

It has been said that, as with most others of my time, my relations with my adoring mother were not—what should I say—normal. Well, they were certainly normal and acceptable (if not entirely proper) for the time. Why don't we just leave it at that? For indeed I sinned enough as it was: drinking and, when both drunk and sober, sleeping with eager girls; gluttony, frivolity. And the songs we sang! They could make a troubadour feel ashamed.

How could I tell that one day I, that dissolute unworthy, would be canonized? Had I been told that I would be crowned king of debauchery—that I would have believed. But a saint! Destiny sometimes speaks loudly, and sometimes very softly. But, yes, in spite of everything I did, I had intimations about my vocation very early on. What is destiny if not God's will working through one's character, enabling it to be acted out?

And I was very competitive; wanting desperately to be first among my friends in everything that we did. I had to run the fastest; drink the most; dance the longest; sleep the least; throw a stone the farthest.

Scene 2

[On no. 2, Francis's companions assemble with him in the town square, Francis now in his stylish, youthful attire]

Friends

Francis! Francis! Come, have you forgotten? Today Assisi celebrates the feast of St. Nicholas. And, as the bishop practices on this one day the virtue of humility, we take over his duties. You are elected to be *l'episcopello*, the boy bishop. Here is your miter; here is your crosier.

[Followed by a processional of his friends, Francis circles the stage and assumes the chair of the bishop. Francis and his friends act out what is said by the chorus.]

Chorus
>   This day the young people
>   Played their roles
>   More fervently than ever before.
>   They ordered food
>   And ravenously consumed it.
>   Girls appeared and soon
>   There was a clamorous orgy
>   Songs and dances
>   Fornications
>   Until everyone was exhausted.

Scene 3

>   *[On no. 1, Francis as a salesman in his father's
>   clothing store, is waiting on a customer, showing him
>   various silks]*

Chorus
>   Francis' father, Bernardone
>   A successful merchant
>   Sold only the finest cloth
>   In the latest fashion.
>   Francis was a gifted salesman
>   Francis was a dandy
>   Who had exquisite taste.
>   Young noblemen eagerly parted
>   With their purses
>   To look as good as he did.
>   Bernardone grew rich
>   The poor became poorer
>   Dressed in rags
>   They shivered in the cold
>   And starved.
>   Unrest, turmoil, revolt
>   Was in the air.
>   In Picardy and Flanders
>   In Milan and elsewhere

Upheavals were already occurring.
There were Cathars and
Brothers of the Free Spirit
There were all manner of religious
Who now made a virtue of poverty.
The bishops grew fat
The people were down to the bone
Beggars were everywhere
And one appeared before Francis
Who was now fourteen, a man
And Francis did something
For which he was forever
Regretful.
  [A beggar in rags enters Bernadones's store]

Beggar
  Alms, alms—for the love of God.

Francis
  Go away! You are filthy! Can't you see I am busy?
    *[Francis continues to show silks to his customer as the
    beggar, downcast, leaves. But then suddenly Francis
    abandons his customer and runs out of the store after
    the beggar. Francis voice is heard off-stage]*
  Forgive me! Forgive me! Here take this money. Take the
  entire purse.

Chorus
  Francis, Francis
  Your true character was beginning
  To show.
  Still with famine
  Spreading throughout the land
  You and your friends feasted
  You and your friends played
  Like irresponsible children.
  But then one day you met a simpleton
  Who threw his cloak on the ground
  Before you and hailed

"O king of youth!
O prince of darkness!
Walk over my cloak."
The simpleton then prophesied:
"You shall receive many
Magnificent honors
From those among us who are
Faithful."
He went on to say:
"Be not deceived. I am indeed
what you see I am
But then you don't see now
What I can see.
You shall be honored."
You were shaken by his prophecy.
Who wouldn't be?
But there were many things that needed
To happen first.
A little savage war was waged
Between Assisi and Perugia
And you, with your youthful
Your zestful spirit, joined with
The knights of Assisi
Who were, however, no match
For those from Perugia.
The battle was lost
You were imprisoned
With those of your companions
Who, like yourself, had not
Been slaughtered on the field.

Scene 4

> *[On no. 1, Francis is in a dank prison cell; his fellow prisoners, dispirited, are lying about. Francis is singing.]*

Francis

> O once I knew a maiden bare
> Who called to me
> And-

Knight

> How can you sing when we rot here? It is cold enough to freeze the voice. Our despair is enough to dry up the heart, as well as other organs. Can't you smell the stink of those of us who are dying? Indeed, those of us who are already dead?

Francis

> Why I am so happy in this miserable place—with sickness, dejection, defeat? Because, I think, someday I shall be loved and adored.

Knight

> You are mad.

Francis

> Yes. I am going crazy: but I'm not sure whether it is a madness of this world or of another.

Knight

> Assuredly it is of this world.

Francis

> Sometimes I rejoice in the memories of my wanton ways; the young women, the dancing, the drinking. At other times I rejoice in knowing that this was not enough and that some day I shall have a better way.

Chorus

> After two years
> Francis, still suffering delusions
> So his companions believed
> Francis in poor health
> Maybe tuberculosis
> Was ransomed out of prison
> And returned home

Where he was looked after
With great affection
By his adoring mother.
Half-heartedly he then resumed
His old ways.
And then he actually became a knight
A rather sorry one at that.
   [Francis, on no. 3]

Francis

I wanted glory. Who doesn't? Only I wanted it too strongly.
The crusades! Who could resist the appeal? We would
reconquer Jerusalem. Deliver it from the infidels. Restore
the honor of Christendom. My father, generous as ever
with me, if only with me, outfitted me magnificently with
the finest armor, a grand horse, and a squire to carry my
shield. I wore a cloak embroidered with gold. O this frail
body so grandly, and heavily, adorned.

Chorus

And then a strange thing happened
Strange at this time
Not, of course, later.
Francis came upon a shabbily dressed knight
A knight who had lost everything in the war
A knight humiliated and rejected
And Francis gave him his expensive cloak
And his carefully crafted weapons
So that the knight would be restored.
Francis with his squire
Continued on to Spoleto
From where Francis was to go
No further.

Scene 5

   *[Francis, on no. 1, is alone in a semi-darkened room,
   standing, looking upward]*

Voice

Francis. What are you going to do?

Francis

I shall be an excellent knight. I shall gain glory. And someday I shall have a beautiful princess.

Voice

And that will be enough?

Francis

I shall be wealthy, with all that wealth brings.

Voice

Who is able to give the most: a master or his servant?

Francis

The master, of course.

Voice

But then why do you abandon the master and follow only servants?

Francis [confused]

What would you have me do?

Voice

Return home—and you will then be told what you must do.

Chorus

And so Francis
Now twenty-five
Returned home
He sold his horse
And its trappings
He bought some simple clothes
And presented himself before
His outraged father.
Money was wasted
But more importantly

The hope was lost that
Through Francis
Bernadone would himself become
Something grand.
O this son!
This pathetic knight!
Returning home before even
Reaching the battlefield
Because he heard a voice!
But Francis was accepted once again
By his freedom-loving friends.
Francis was still their leader
Until that extraordinary event occurred.

Scene 6

> *[Francis shown, as in the opening of Act I on no. 2 in his trance, announcing]*

Francis

I shall marry the noblest and the most beautiful lady ever to be seen.

ACT III

Chorus

Francis had his brotherhood
Men sworn to poverty
The Friars Minor, the lesser brothers,
He called them.
Francis went to Rome in 1209
To meet with Pope Innocent III
To secure Innocent's approval
Of his brotherhood.
Dressed like a beggar
Francis had his audience
With the Pope.

But with one look at Francis
Innocent said:
"Brother, go herd pigs.
You look like them.
Roll in the dunghill with them
Preach to them and offer
Them your rule."
And Francis did so.
And then returned to Pope Innocent III.

Scene 1

*[Francis, on no. 1, covered with mud and slime, is
standing before the Pope, who remained seated]*

Innocent

You are determined, I see, to teach everyone humility. But
how can we can condone a brotherhood of those who,
although loyal to the Church, follow only the Gospel? We
already have various and numerous orders of monks. Why
not join one of them? Or have a new order of your own—
with proper rules, organization, and the necessary money
to carry out your mission, without all this unseemly
begging and deprivation? We must all use common sense.
The Church does indeed need renewal. We must recover a
spiritual depth; not, however, by renouncing everything,
but only that which is excessive. God's work requires
moderation: neither luxury nor poverty.

[Francis remains silent]

Innocent

You think that I am speaking only as a politician—and not
from the spirit. Very well, I will dream about it. You too
look for further counsel in your dreams. Let it be there
that we learn of your destiny.

Chorus

No further thinking by the Pope
No further reflection on whether to grant

Approval of Francis' brotherhood
Pope Innocent III dreamed about it.
And why not?
Dreams tell us
About what was.
Dreams tell us
About what we want to have be
And what we fear might be.
Dreams tell us too
About what should be.
Dreams disclose His will.
And so Innocent dreamed.
And Francis dreamed.
The Pope saw a monk
Who looked like a beggar
Leaning against an old church
Supporting it
Preventing it from falling.
Francis saw a very poor woman
Living in the desert
With many children
Who had been sired by a rich king.
The woman told her grown sons
"Go to the palace and look
For your father, the king."
They did so
And the king, acknowledging
That they were indeed his sons
Took care of them.
Innocent and Francis
Related their dreams to each other.
And then the Pope granted his approval
Of Francis' Brotherhood
With its rules only
Of obedience and poverty.
He allowed them to preach
But he gave none of this
In writing.

Scene 2

*[Francis, on no. 1, outdoors in a wooded area, standing
before his followers who are gathered around him]*

Francis

O Friars! Own nothing other than your habit, your cord,
and your trousers. Live in obedience and chastity. Never
be gloomy, even when fasting. Celebrate the liturgy.
Clerics should be treated with respect and should be
followed in everything so long as it is not contrary to what
we believe. Work always in the service of others. No
money is ever to be received. Never speak to a woman
alone. Don't ride horseback or have an animal of any kind.
Be humble. Be patient. Strive for perfect simplicity.

Scene 3

*[On no. 1, demons wearing hideous masks and
dressed in brightly colored robes, jumping around
Francis who is standing immobile, in dim light]*

Demons

We've got you Francis. We've got you.
     [while uttering eerie sounds]
Here is a woman for you.
     *[With vulgar gestures, demon imitates a large-
     breasted woman]*
Look at this soft bed with silk sheets
O you want that too!
You want to kill someone
But first watch him suffer
Excruciatingly.
Here, here are some snakes to play with
Ah, you are filling-up with hatred
For the lepers?
O no!
Not for him!

Scene 4

> *[Francis, on no. 1, in Franciscan habit, is confronted by a boy leading his father who is blind]*

Boy
Someone told me you can help me. Can help my father.

Francis
Who told you?

Boy
It was a voice.

Francis
What did it say?

Boy
That you could help me. Could help my father who is blind.

Francis
In those words?

Boy
It said: "Go to him who considers himself the least worthy of men."

Francis
How did you know that was me?

Boy
Everyone knows that, O Francis. But of course no one believes it.

Francis
I am the least worthy. And you are blessed.
> *[Francis places his hand across the man's eyes and holds it there intently for a short time. As he removes his hand, the father cries out.]*

Father
Light! There is light! I can see! O my son, I can see!

[The boy falls before Francis' feet. Francis picks him up and embraces him.]

Francis

All praise to the Lord!
[Simultaneous with above, Francis on no. 3]

Francis

Pace e bene—I called out wherever we went. Peace and joy. I wanted to bring everyone face to face with my Lord. We made a little settlement at Rivo Torto, where we gladly endured many tribulations. We cared for the lepers. We begged for our food. We prayed and we were filled with peace and joy.

We moved then to La Portiuncula, a lovely place lent to us by the good Benedictines. Everyone worked. Everyone prayed. Many miracles occurred—and hundreds came to us, including Clare. Clare, Clare, wonderful Clare!

She was a beautiful woman, twelve years younger—but many years wiser—than me. Wealthy, aristocratic, she wanted to be married to the Lord. She came to me for counsel—and for argument. We met secretly in the woods. We loved one another deeply, without touching. We loved one another in Christ.

Scene 5

[Francis and Clare, on no. 1, in a clearing in the woods. It is night-time]

Clare

I come to you for help. I have listened to you preach and I have watched you pray. The love you have is the love I want for my own. I tremble when I think of your being with Him. I want nothing but Him alone.

Francis

You have everything now that the world cherishes. Beauty and richness, manner and charm. I can give you nothing.

Clare

Which is what I want.

Francis

I don't believe you. I don't believe a woman can renounce everything.

Clare

Is it because we are able to reproduce and nurture that you envy us, and then resent and disbelieve us? You regard yourselves as superior and, although assuredly you are stronger, at least in the short run, you are nevertheless weak. For what does someone who is truly strong have to fear from someone else? And you do fear us and then abhor us.

Francis

We don't fear you. We fear ourselves.

Clare

But then why identify yourselves with spirit and mind, and us with matter and body—and then go so far as to think of us as your property?

Francis

By our Rule we own nothing—let alone another human being. But, yes, as men, we do fear our lower self and we do see women as that which causes us to fall into it.

Clare

But then we are only the victim, not the cause of your temptation and misery. Why can't all of us, both men and women, be children of God?

Francis

Am I then to be your father?

Clare

No. I am asking to be your partner in a very special kind of love. And why do you presume that the Lord is to be shaped in a man's hairy image alone? Especially when the shaping is at our expense? Did He not proclaim our equality? Are we not among the downtrodden whom He intended to enter first into the kingdom?

Francis

But not all women are oppressed, any more than all men are free. Everyone, man and woman alike, is, however, lost without Him. And by "Him," yes, we do mean God and Son of God, for that is how it has been said. But we also allow—do we not?—for the female in Spirit: indeed, as I have been told, some might say as the Holy Spirit itself. Also, we affirm, we do not deny, the qualities of caring, of nurturing, of mutuality; we honor them as among the most worthy for a human being to possess—for did He not possess them in abundance?

Clare

But, don't you see, that only gives a so-called feminine character to what remains a dominant masculine image. Certainly every human being should strive to be at once intelligent and caring, strong and sensitive, without these being thought of as either masculine or feminine. And each person should strive to be these in his and her own way, with full equality.

Francis

But Mary, Mother of God, Virgin, forever pure: do we not celebrate her as well?

Clare

Mary was blessed, assuredly. But you use her to degrade all other women; separating her out from us in order to see us more sharply as the source of sin. Mary, in your eyes, is the new Eve; but one who this time is totally obedient.

Francis

I am not learned. I am not a theologian. But I see Mary as disclosing the Church's redeemed body. Mary symbolizes our spiritual body, in glory. And every kind of relationship, whether with family, with government, with church, calls for—does it not?—certain inequalities. Different people have different kinds of responsibilities. Jesus himself, although overthrowing encrusted and privileged power, certainly recognized that. And our Church clearly embodies it.

Clare

I am not speaking about hierarchies as such. My point is that if Christ redeems all of us in the wholeness of our own individual being, then why should men and women not be full partners, without fear, in all orders of life?

Francis

Christ was not concerned with our having happy relationships between equal partners, men and women. He was concerned only with the spiritual redemption of mankind. He suffered no fear, of man or of woman.

Clare

Anyway, I think, dear Francis, that maybe there is a part of you that is frightened by me, a woman, or just by me. But I yearn only to be His bride. I will love you—I already do—in your love of Him.

Francis

Is it possible? Can we love one another in the Spirit alone? Can we be spiritual and not carnal partners?

Clare

Yes. Yes. It is possible. It will be.

Chorus

A daughter of poverty
Dressed in rags
Clare walked the streets
Unrecognized
Begging for food
Joyful, at peace.
She met again with Francis—
And let us not forget
That Francis himself once said
"Don't canonize me too soon

I am still capable of fathering children"
And when tempted by the flesh
Would hurl himself
In the midst of winter
Into a ditch filled with ice—
Francis, with his own hands
Cut off Clare's beautiful hair
And led her in the vows of poverty.
And so the brotherhood
Would have women:
Nuns of the Convents of the Poor Clares.

Scene 6

[On no. 2, five friars are playing ball with some children. A few townspeople in background look on in gleeful astonishment.]

Friar

Here, see if you catch this one.
[Throws a ball high in the air. Several children rush together to catch it, but just as it is about to reach them another Friar grabs it from the air.]

Friar

Oh, is this for me?

Children

That's not fair. He's taller than we are.

Friar

But I'm not. Throw the ball again.
[The ball is thrown again to the children together with the short friar and this time it is caught by one of the children. Laughing, the children throw it to each other, keeping it away from the friars who are playfully chasing after them. A friar manages to intercept it and throws it to another friar, upon whom the children all jump.]

Scene 7

[Francis on no. 3]

Francis

How much misery must the world bear before one is willing to leave it? Plagues, famine, corruption; emperors fighting popes, city against city; town against town. Yet our task is not so much to leave the world as to make it worthy of its having been God's creation.
[On no. 1, with birds fluttering about—simultaneously with above on no. 3]

Francis

You dress simply, which is good. And you dress alike, which is smart. You have the great sky, the beautiful openness to fly around in. Your sweet singing is heard everywhere. Remember how God provides for you. Know that you are blessed. Offer your praise to the Lord!

Chorus

Elias joined the brotherhood
Elias who would one day be
Its ruler
Elias who would one day
Come to ruin
Elias humble and proud
A man of love and a man of power
Born in Assisi, a contemporary
Of Francis
Devoted to Francis
And to his own ambitions.
Pope Innocent III died
And Cardinal Savelli became
Pope Honorius III.
And Plans were laid
For a Fifth Crusade.
Francis was determined
To join it in order to meet

And to convert the Sultan of Egypt.
Cardinal Ugolino, advisor, confidant
Of Francis, did not oppose him.
A crowd of brothers accompanied
Francis to Anconia from where
He was to sail.
But there was room on the boat
Only for twelve.
So Francis asked a young child passing by
To point to those who should make the trip.
Let the child express God's will!
And Francis met Malik al-Kamil
Sultan of Egypt
A man of learning
A man of refinement
Certainly no fool
Or degenerate was he.

Scene 8

[Francis, on no. 1, with one companion standing aside in the background, and Malik al-Kamil in a room in the sultan's palace]

Francis

I am here to convert you—and thereby also to end this bloody carnage. I come not as an emissary, but on my own, as leader of a brotherhood dedicated to peace and to love.

Malik

You are welcome. At first I thought you were here in disguise in order to surrender to us. Quite a few of you have done so. We would make a good Muslim of you. But why, pray tell me, should I become a Christian? What do you offer that my Islam doesn't?

Francis

Christ, who died for our sins on the cross; Son of God, with God and the Holy Spirit, a Trinity, is the one true being who will redeem the world. Our religion is one of love, of repentance, of salvation.

Malik

I see little enough of love, let alone of repentance and salvation, among that motley gang calling themselves crusaders, or among their greedy, barbarous leaders; among whom, as I understand, are some bishops of your church. As least we are honest. We don't carry on about love. We simply and rightly use the sword when it is necessary. O yes, we too have our pure men of God; and we honor them and adore their songs—in their place.

Francis

Our Church, which is of course imperfect, has a sacred mission. It is a necessary means to, and does in principle, embody the Truth.

Malik

But are there not many ways to the Truth? Some among us say that the Divine is absolute simplicity, about which nothing finally can properly be said. But we also have our book, the Qu'ran, which you probably have never seen or heard; and we have our laws, rules, principles, and prohibitions in considerable abundance.

Francis

Yes, there are undoubtedly several religions, including yours, which have holy books and learned scholars to interpret them; which have rules of conduct and sacred places and ways of worship—but Christianity alone offers salvation. With us you can be saved; without us you are lost—condemned to at best an incompleteness.

Malik

What proof have you that I am now lost and that your religion can save me?

Francis

We have His word.

Malik

But that is not a proof.

Francis

Faith in His word brings a conviction that demands no
further proof.

Malik

In order then to believe, one must already believe! No,
your religion is not for me; it is not for us. You be a good
Christian; I will be a good Muslim. And let us hope that
one day we can live in peace together.

Chorus

Francis failed to convert
The Sultan
Francis would have to convert
Only professed Christians
Sunk in this world.
Back home. Honorius III announced plans
For Francis' brotherhood.
It would be made into an order
With proper rules and property.
Francis was in declining health
The brotherhood was growing
Francis asked the Pope to appoint
Ugolino, friend and advisor, to be
Protector of the Friars Minor.
Francis was growing blind.
Elias, devoted to Francis
Ambitious, clever and bold
Was appointed Minister General
Of what was already becoming
Another order
With thousands of members.
Elias governed and
Francis wandered.

Scene 9

*[Francis, on no. 1, at La Verna, a cave in the hill, on
one knee, his arms extended]*

Francis

O Lord! Let me suffer
As you have suffered.
Let your agony be mine
The nails, the lance
Tearing into the flesh
The pain unspeakable
Your mouth burning
Your heart pounding
Let me tortured
With you!

*[A piercing light strikes Francis; blood issues from his
hands and his right side. Francis remains still, in
ecstasy. Chorus simultaneously with this depiction.]*

Chorus

Francis had his stigmata
Francis was dying
Brother Leo knew of his wounds
And tenderly cared for him.
Francis was dying
He would enter the Kingdom
And would forever praise the Lord.
He composed his "Canticle of Brother Sun"
Whose last verses are:
"Happy those who endure in peace
    By you, Most High. they will be crowned.
All praise be yours, my Lord, through Sister Death,
    From whose embrace no mortal can escape.
Woe to those who die in mortal sin!
    Happy those She finds doing Your will!
    The second death can do no harm to them.
Praise and bless my Lord, and give Him thanks
    And serve Him with great humility."

Scene 10

[Francis, on no. 1, lying on a cot; Clare at his bedside with Francis' father behind her]

Francis

Clare, is that you? I can barely see you.

Clare

Yes, I am with you. And your father is here too.

Francis

My father?

Clare

Yes, Bernadone. He wanted desperately to see you.

Father

I am old and perhaps now a little wiser. You are revered everywhere; not as a nobleman—which is what I foolishly wanted—but as a saint, which I still find hard to believe. Anyway, although I am your father, I ask for your blessing.

Francis

You certainly have my blessing—but not as my father. You have my blessing as you too are a child of God.

Clare

Don't be so harsh, Francis. A natural father will always have a special relationship with his son. Don't you see how difficult it is for Bernardone to come before you?

Francis

It will be more difficult for him when he comes before the Lord. I am not his judge. And I have no special relationship to him; nor do I have any malice toward him. But let me be alone with you Clare for a minute or two.

[Bernardone leaves sorrowfully]

Francis

Well, Clare, my work here is finished. How are the sisters? Are they behaving themselves?

Clare

They are fine. And you still speak as though we were not to be taken seriously.

Francis

Forgive me. I speak only in jest. I know that we will soon be apart.

Clare

You will remain in my heart forever.

Francis

We did live and love as partners in Spirit.

Clare

Yes, as partners—if not completely equal ones!
    [They laugh together]

Chorus

And so Francis prepared his last testament
Filled with exhortations
A severe document
Born of love.
In it he declared:
"Do not interpret my words. They are uttered
Plainly and simply, and you should live by them
Doing good to the very end."

The doctors operated on Francis
They cut his eyes and
Branded his body
Already disfigured and wasted.
All, of course, to no avail.

Part 3

Dialogues, Monologues, and Discussions

On the Dark Night
of the Soul

She said:

You lament, you complain, you plead, you pray. Why not do something today that will change the world, however so slightly?

He said:

You don't understand.

She said:

Wanting to please you, I came here; away from friends, far from family. You have now seen new faces and novel things. Why not then do something different?

He said:

I am still not here.

She said:

You have to be somewhere or other. It is not for you, for me, for anyone to be nowhere at all.

He said:

If the wind ceased to blow the leaves about and no one cared, then you would understand how empty everything can become.

She said:

I only know that you like your meals on time and that if you expect me to prepare them you'll have to do as others do—and forget.

Questions Not Tending toward Edification

She asked and declared:

Who if not we, implacable still would deny this ubiquitous silence; this swollen distended mystery which, unremittingly, flows through the subtle intricacies of our every awareness?

O infinite variations of pure night of white light and white snow! Delicious diadems! Seraphic glow! And you, unable to know, unable to feel, your senses in rivalry, your consciousness chaotic, the pervasive force playing beneath transient appearances. The lines in a leaf stretch and embrace the infinite space, while you, replete with insensate deceit, worship man-made beauties.

O the body was born to delight in the splendor of twilight and the radiance of a cool spring's morning!

He responded and asked:

Yes, there lies a whiteness sole in the darkened night: quivering pale white light within light while you, with your intensities from ecstasy to ennui, transfigure that silence into senseless sound.

O infinite subtleties, nuances and intricacies of mind! O visions of the soul lost and forgotten in this endless journey, in this incessant movement into persons only distantly related to me. Why can't we in our fugitive sleep enter the region of untouched space and remain there simply, embracing its essence? Why must we, moment to moment, endure this cycle of misery and suffering, as though life were to be known only through dying while living surrounded by a terrible mystery?

Freudian Parenthood

Mother and Son

He said:

Mother—may you someday rot in hell—for trying to seduce me when I was only thirteen!

Did you know or care what you were doing? However you answer you condemn yourself, for you condemned me to a life-long affliction. Although, of course, nothing transpired, you were forever a threat, maybe a promise, surely a possibility by which every other relationship with a woman was measured.

She said:

My son, I always knew you would have whatever you were determined to have, and from me you learned what it means to avoid temptation. So quit your moaning and be grateful, for what you have learned is certainly a rare gift indeed.

Father and Daughter

She said:

Why did you abandon me and go away with my mother, when all the time I knew, as you knew, that it was me whom—Oh, I can't say it, I can't really believe it—but nevertheless know it to be true.

He said:

No, but yes, and maybe yes and no—anyway, you are wrong in a very basic way and so get on with your own business of living. What else can a father say?

Mother and Daughter

The mother said:

Why don't we understand one another? Why this rejection—when all along I only wanted what was best for you? Look at Mary, and then remember who you are.

The daughter replied:

Mary! Good heavens! Would that I were His bride rather than His virgin mother!

Father and Son

The son said:

I needed your protection and your example of what it means to be a man. These you gave me, but nothing else. Did you really believe that was sufficient?

The father replied:

I had other matters—indeed, the whole world—to attend to.

Modes of Being

Before the youthful turning and the decisive choice
The suffering and the senseless choosing
And after the choices, though ever-recurring,
We lament
We rejoice.

We become the roles that we play while to us other beings are only and always just themselves, as concentrations of limitations. And so we announce: "Freedom is just for those who can become and are not already bound."

And so, with not just a little tumidity, we proclaim our superiority!

māyā: substituting the mind for reality and taking that world as real.
māyā: the fact of *discontinuity*.
māyā: the attraction of the beginningless performance, until it can no longer be seen in the blazing light.

And the many-faced and many-armed god sees in all directions: but still from a fixed position.

The silence which is just an absence is oppressive. But when it is a presence it overwhelms and is joyful.

93

There is that which cannot be said because there is no distance there between speaking and being.

Silence is the place for listening.

yin-yang: there is no active or passive, aggressive or receptive, dominant or compliant *dichotomy* of being. For each mode becomes the other and death is just that state of being on the other side of living.

But you are forgetting the wind! Yes, look there, at the wind!

Questions

The full moon shimmered on the unanimous sea, while we, as if taking exception to it, quarreled the night away.

But then—don't you see?—someone, somewhere, at this moment, is dancing!

If there is no time, then I am everywhere present—unless, when there is no time there is no 'I'.

But have you ever lost yourself in a blood-drenched, sunsetting sky?

Illusions

The stick bends in the water: it is in that upon which it is reflected.

The white light dances on the moon-lit sea, illuminating its own image.

While we, with our memories, objectify ourselves and call that a world.

The greatest discipline and practice is required to be nothing, and yet people speak of him as being powerless, as though he is powerful who merely exercises control over others.

A few mirrors rightly placed can reflect images without number, as though the single object before them had become infinitely many. Creation by reflective multiplication! How simple—and insubstantial.

We refuse to recognize our own condition even when presented with overwhelming evidence regarding it, if the recognition is of the sort that calls for a dramatic shift in one's values and expectations.

The clinging to the habitual, the power of the illusion.

Religious Psychology

Religion, necessarily, is psychological—being, as it is, an affair of consciousness: the remaining question is whether or not religion is reducible to psychology. Freud thought so— while assuming that religion itself could be reduced to a popular form of Judeo-Christian theism and that psychology could here consist in giving a genetic account of a person's religiosity in terms of basic (infantile) needs, fears, and attachments, with the aim, finally, of liberating the person from them.[1]

William James: "By their fruits ye shall know them, not by their roots."

Theism, at some levels, might indeed be prompted by fright and, as James indicated, by any number of "nervous" pathological conditions. But as James also asked: "When we think certain states of mind superior to others, is it ever because of what we know concerning their organic antecedents?"[2] Spirituality, at its highest level, is precisely the overcoming of all fear or, one might better say, its utter elimination, and bears a significance incommensurable with whatever might be put forward as a causal or genetic explanation of it.

Freud would have the repressed contents of the unconscious play a central role in human experience; indeed, in transformed ways they become the very content of much of that experience. On the other hand, Freud is singularly uninterested in religious experience, assuming as he does that religion ("the ordinary man and his religion—the only religion that ought to bear the name"[3]) consists essentially in a credo—a set of dogmas whose belief in is demanded by the particular religion. Accordingly, Freud's "explanations" of the content of religion are focused on showing how these believed-in dogmas are "illusions." "[Religious] dogmas," he writes, "are not the residue of experience or the final result of reflection; they are illusions, fulfillments of the oldest, strongest and most insistent wishes of mankind."[4]

Allowing that an "illusion need not be necessarily false, that is to say, unrealizable or incompatible with reality,"[5] in short, a delusion, Freud nevertheless asserts that "some of them [religious doctrines] are so improbable, so very incompatible with everything we have laboriously discovered about the reality of the world, that we may compare them—taking into account the psychological differences—to delusions."[6]

For Feuerbach, who philosophically argues a stronger case, a religious vision would be less of a recollection than an extreme case of amnesia, a self-emptying by way of a projection of one's fears and hopes on to reality. This exercise of archaic imagination which peoples the world with gods and demons gives definition, then, and supposed meaning to one's deep-felt sense of helplessness and dependency. A religious vision, in short, is the self made perceptible to itself—unknowingly. For Feuerbach, religion is only an internal dramaturgy.

Spirituality begins, as it were, from at least two different possible "attitudes": (1) from an anguished awareness of a root inadequacy of oneself and the world; that is, a sense of disquiet, of unfulfillment, of incompleteness within a world circumscribed by practical necessities and without apparent purpose; and (2) from a joyous awareness of a compelling power and value that draws one spontaneously to it and as it becomes one's own most valued state of being.

Both origins, being modes of awareness, are psychological; but they can be said to be so only if at the same time they are acknowledged to be ontological and axiological as well.

Religious experience, in its immense variety, can be regarded as *performances*—hence "scripted," and, as with emotionality in general, in both psycho-biological and social-cultural terms. Spiritual enlightenment, on the other hand, knows nothing of "scripts" and, being endurable, is, in principle, non-repeatable.

It is not so much doubt concerning the "existence of God" but the awareness of the ever-present possibility of self-deception that properly haunts religious consciousness. The self-deception involved here is not the usual pedestrian form of there being a marked disparity between one's announced self and the person one quite clearly shows oneself to be to others, rather it is a "root" self-deception, the confounding of what is still very much one's own self with reality. Self-deception here means the possibility that religious consciousness is only an attenuated self-consciousness in the form of an extreme expression of ego.

For those of a critical bent of mind the awareness of the ever-present possibility of this form of self-deception is not simply a doubting subsequent to a religious experience, but an attitude that reaches into the very heart of that experience and prevents thereby its consummation. How is this gloom to be dispelled?

The answer is simple; its realization extraordinarily difficult.

Notes

1. See his *The Future of an Illusion*, originally published in 1927.

2. William James, *Varieties of Religious Experience: A Study in Human Nature* (New York, London: Longmans, Green and Company, 1902), lecture 1, "Religion and Neurology", p. 13.

3. Sigmund Freud, *Civilization and Its Discontents*, trans. by Joan Riviere (Garden City, New York: Doubleday & Company, Inc., n.d.), p. 14.

4. Freud, *The Future of an Illusion*, trans. by W.D. Robson-Scott (Garden City, New York: Doubleday & Company, Inc., n.d.), p. 51.

5. Ibid., p. 53.

6. Ibid., p. 54.

Enemies, Impediments, and Distractions

The beautiful in nature is a distraction from spirituality whenever we fail to experience it praisefully as mystery and attend to it solely as a source of private satisfaction.

Curiosity is a distraction when it becomes only a way to empowerment.

Obligations which we undertake in order to conform, to be busy, to be recognized, become prime distractions when we justify the undertakings high-mindedly on the grounds that we are thereby fulfilling our social responsibilities.

Sickness and old age—not enemies but distractions which impede one's ability to attend.

. . .

It is not that sexuality as such is an impediment to spirituality, but our inability to keep it from consuming one — which seems to happen more often than not to the ascetic who would "conquer" sexuality at its source as well as to one who is unable to master it on the surface.

Wanting to have the things of the world and striving to be something or other that will be praised by others—and having and being these—are among the most pernicious impediments to the attaining of spiritual consciousness.

Seeing things too clearly and not seeing them at all—both are impediments to the spiritual life.

Institutional religion (the "religions" as organized systems regulating ritual and belief), while apparently providing a needed structure to support most persons' religiosity, serve as a kind of filter, allowing only selective access to the divine and hence become an impediment to unmediated spirituality.

Humility: an impediment when it becomes self-consciously sought for.

The unconscious as inescapably intrusive: the primary impediment to spirituality.

. . .

The most subtle enemy of the spiritual life, it seems, is stupidity. "Stupidity" here does not mean a native deficiency of intellect; quite the contrary, it means a clinging to certain highly developed mental capacities which, if they were properly attended to, would show their own insufficiency. Stupidity is the refusal to acknowledge one's intellectual limitations. It belongs most frequently to those who possess intellectual powers to a high degree. Stupidity is the belief that one can substitute one's own intellect for reality. It thus wraps a person into himself and shuts off a wide range of other mental possibilities. To be stupid is thus to be irrational. And this kind of madness surely forecloses the possibility of realizing a spiritual life.

Stupidity, intellectual arrogance, the little devil within one, paradoxically perhaps, is a form of cowardice, a way of avoiding risk. Let us indeed, it says, build a warm fire in the cave and stay comfortably at home there.

Pride: yes, the cardinal enemy, when it is an attenuated stupidity.

On Moral and Religious Love

Is it not the case that if most of us loved our neighbor as ourself it would be too bad for the neighbor? Self-loathing rather than self-love (in any genuine non-egoistic sense) seems characteristic of *Dasein*. Much work needs to be done before one should have the audacity to love one's neighbor as oneself.

According to Nietzsche, love—Christian love—is born of *ressentiment*, whose source is a thirst for revenge.

The slave revolt in morals begins by rancor turning creative and giving birth to values—the rancor of beings who, deprived of the direct outlet of action, compensate by an imaginary vengeance. All truly noble morality grows out of triumphant self-affirmation. Slave ethics, on the other hand, begins by saying no to an 'outside,' an 'other,' a non-self, and that no is its creative act. This reversal of direction of the evaluating look, this invariable looking outward instead of inward, is a fundamental feature of rancor....

Whereas the noble lives before his own conscience with confidence and frankness...the rancorous person is neither truthful nor ingenuous, nor honest and forthright with himself. His soul squints; his mind loves hide-outs, secret paths, and back doors; everything that is hidden seems to him his own world....

...When a noble man feels resentment, it is absorbed in his instantaneous reaction and therefore does not poison him. Moreover in countless cases where we might expect it, it never arises, while with weak and impotent people it occurs without fail.

(Genealogy of Morals, I, x)

Now apart from Nietzsche's dubious Freudian-like model of the play of instinctual energies (their repression and their subsequently having to express themselves in one way or another) and also apart from his questionable historical account of the nature of Christian love as the triumph of the people of *ressentiment*, Nietzsche's insight into the manner in which the "rancorous person" is so filled with self-hatred—the hatred of his own impotence as disclosed by the strength of others—that he is rendered incapable of love, must be recognized to be profound. Love requires self-assurance and confidence. Religious love is not where the meek reside. Religious love is not for the revenge-driven paranoids of the world. Religious love, as Nietzsche—that repressed Christian with his "excessive brilliance"—knew, is only for the strong.

Agapē: the Hegelian coming home of emotional consciousness.

One ought not to worry about being worthy of being loved, but about being capable of loving. With that capability, the "being loved" follows quite naturally.

"You shall love..."—but love cannot be commanded; it can only be awakened and nourished, allowed to grow and mature.

Is the erotic ever absent from religious devotion? The intense yearning of the aspiring bride of Christ and of the passionate *bhakta* is surely grounded in desire as it motivates them toward the Other. Does it then inform the love that is achieved?

God's love, the theist proclaims, is like but at the same time very much unlike our human love. God's love is free from need, yet it is personal. We, on the other hand, are entirely impersonal when we are free from need.

Spinoza would have us sublimate our ordinary ego-based emotions in an "intellectual love of God"—a passional state of being which is at one with the reason of all things. He rightfully observes that the achievement of this love, this freedom, is as difficult as it is rare.

Do we really want a love that is blind? Or do we want a sensitivity that can make the finest qualitative discriminations? Is it possible to have both at once?

Religious love ought to be a form of play; an activity carried out for its own sake, without expectation of anything in return. It is then that love receives everything.

Persons can, it seems, become players of love from two rather contrary conditions: from their transcending their intense deprivations (usually sexual in nature); from their fulfilling, by becoming a new being, a deeply satisfying interpersonal relationship. In the one case religious love comes from a lack, in the other from an abundance.

The Ironic Gaze

I look at you bemusedly, with a measured incredulity; I look at you as if you were incapable of being aware of yourself. I look at you ironically.

The ironic gaze subdues and overcomes the other, who is the object of its gaze, by denying the other's self-announced importance. Annihilating the presumed eternal values the other proclaims, the ironist renders that other comical. Through its exaggerated and duplicitous attentiveness, the ironic gaze tries to get the other to see itself as an enigma and not as a completed thing.

An enormous power thus resides in the look of the ironist, a power, he believes, that may transform pretense into reality.

It would be inappropriate to look ironically upon nature, for nature simply is in its owness and cannot be other than it is in its actuality. Nature makes no claims that need to be shattered.

An ironic gaze has nothing positive in itself to offer, as it can only say to the other "You—although I am superior to you—are as empty as me." It can, then, at its best, be only therapeutic. It can never as such be constructive.

107

Belonging

There is a belonging with others and the world that is natural and ego-bound (it announces: I am one among many of the same kind and am so recognized and respected by others), and there is a belonging which comes with the overpowering of alienation from being. The one offers a certain ease and comfort, the other bliss.

Belonging is relational, but when it is blissful it is also playful; a self that is present to itself in virtue of its recognition that from its non-separation from being it belongs to others and the world in the essential mode of non-attachment, of freedom.

Belonging, when it is blissful, is not possessed by a self that is simply pleased with itself in its relations to others and the world; a successful self, a proud person; it is rather what possesses a self as it celebrates its finding where it properly belongs, in spirit.

Belonging, when it is blissful, is a kind of homecoming, a return and yet a re-making of the enduring that is always new: it is a renewal, a finding of the self as it is taken hold of in love.

A self that truly belongs says "I am that, and that is me"—not as an acquisition but as a mutual appropriation. Belonging then becomes a binding that is freely constituted. It is the achievement of harmony, indeed, through love, of that peace 'that passeth all understanding."

Bronze statue of Parvati, standing. Prov.: Southeast India. Height: 27³/₈ inches. Photo courtesy of the Metropolitan Museum of Art, Cora Timken Burnett Collection of Persian Miniatures and other Persian Art objects, Bequest of Cora Timken Burnett, 1956.

On Images of Gods and Goddesses

Let us regard *Pārvatī*, the daughter of the mountains (*parvata*), consort of the great god Śiva. "Impressed with her asceticism and her devotion to him, Śiva was persuaded by the gods to marry her in order to create a divine child who would destroy the demon Tārakāsura....In Hindu culture, Pārvatī, who is a reincarnation of Satī, is regarded as the divine exemplar of the ideal wife."[1]

Śiva, Hindu mythology holds, is powerless without the *śakti*, energy, afforded by *Pārvatī*. Looking at *Pārvatī*, the Hindu sees at once a world imbued with spiritual/sexual energy and an ideal possibility to be fulfilled. And when the seeing is so intense as to become complete, *Pārvatī* herself is no longer seen—only the *śakti* she embodies. The image, in short, is no longer a representation but a reality—a spiritual presence. For the devotee, *Pārvatī* has worked her magic.

Although this particular illustration of *Pārvatī* is taken from Chola art of a very high artistic quality, Curt Maury's description of the encounter of a typical Hindu villager with his god or goddess is very much to the point:

> Barely visible in the dark hollow of the altar niche, often crudely formed by untutored hands and devoid of artistic merit, it embodies all meaning, all reality, to the devotee. At once terrifyingly awesome and

110

sublimely beautiful to him, this vague, sometimes weird and occasionally unidentifiable shape radiates the magic of a world beyond and its transcendence, of which for moments he becomes a part.[2]

Images of gods and goddesses fill something of that divine *absence* in the world. They call for the presence of that which is otherwise undisclosed.

Verbal as well as pictorial images, when functioning as religious representations rather than as artistic presentations, are clearly a central part of religious language. They set creedal content, and in many ways more effectively than doctrinal words, fixing in the mind, as they do, various features of the divine extolled in the given tradition. As iconoclasts throughout history have known, however, the downside is that they can fix that content all too strongly and bring about, if not outright idolatry, a determination of divine being which is antithetical to its nature.

The problem, then, is that of understanding the religious import of images of gods and goddesses in the context of the iconoclast's question "If indeed we are created in God's image, how can our images witness to Him?" or that of apophatic theology which emphasizes the incommensurability between God and any representation of Him/Her and thus regards images of the divine as at once unnecessary and preposterous; and also in the context of what might well be an aesthetician's assertion that "images ought to invite rather than determine, but that is the task of art to accomplish rather than (liturgical or sacramental) religion as such."

As in art, so in religion; it hardly makes sense to speak of the truth of an image in terms of some mimetic conception or other. An image does not and cannot imitate what it purportedly stands for; it can only be a representation of "it," and like all representations it is presented in a certain conventional vocabulary and is informed throughout with cultural expectations, standards and values.

Religious images, then, are not so much "interpreted" as they are simply recognized by the devotee and are responded to as such. They make immediate to feeling what is otherwise remote to reason. Images of the divine function always intersubjectively and thus strengthen a community of the faithful by focusing attention and emotion on a commonly received awareness.

The (sophisticated) believer, then, can on one level agree with a rationalist who might declare that religious images do not so much point to a spiritual reality as they disclose various religious conceptions of its maker. It is the conception rather than the reality which is embodied in the image. Images of the gods and goddesses are less representations of actual divine personae as they are human contrivances which show presumed features and attributes of the divine as conceptualized in a tradition. On another level, however, the believer can still maintain that the efficacy of divine images lay in their being regarded precisely as *symbolic* representations of divine personae, for only then can they become numinous presences. Divine images, in short, might be acknowledged to be human presentations, as are all symbolic formulations, but they nevertheless in faith become sources of genuine religious response. And it is surely the case that the more abstract the image or representation (e.g., the Cross), the less immediately present and the more remote or symbolic it becomes—which is to say, the response of the believer to it rests primarily on the associations triggered by it rather than on its immediate sensuous content. This is, of course, always a matter of degree, for much of the efficacy of pictorial images *religiously* speaking rests precisely on those same associations. It is necessary to emphasize "religiously" here in order to distinguish it from the aesthetic dimensions or role of images in works of art where their power is essentially inherent or intrinsic to their formal expressiveness. At the same time, some images in religion—especially those of the "terrible" (Kālī wearing her garland of skulls)—can have an immediate impact in terms of their inherent power combined with their symbolic associations. Totemic images of the protective deities in all cultures can have this terrifying appeal.

Western theologians of a rationalistic bent have nevertheless often assumed that the use of divine images is primarily for the sake of the illiterate; that they are at best substitutes for the real teaching. But this attitude only reflects the too-sharp distinction between intellect and imagination that has characterized so much of classical and early modern thought and that disallows the possibility that the imaginative can contribute directly to the cognitive.

Feminist theologians (e.g., Rosemary Ruether) have certainly understood this and emphasize accordingly the impact of the patriarchal character of the divine image in the Judeo-Christian tradition, of "the normative image of transcendent ego in the male God image"[3] and seek to restore, or otherwise incorporate, imagery appropriate to their own experience as women. They hope thereby to undermine the values and attitudes which have contributed to the subordination of women in the tradition. Important as this might be, the positive task they face is extremely difficult, for the very nature of religious imagery is such that it arises, as does mythology itself, in a rather spontaneous, unselfconscious manner. Its origin and development is organic to a community and hence usually evolves only within considerable historical experience.

Returning to the iconoclast's question "If indeed we are created in God's image, how can our images witness to Him?," Gerardus van der Leeuw notes that, "as Posidonius maintained, the human body contains the *logos* and is therefore worthy of representing God. In the Byzantine dispute about images, further, this was rendered yet more profound by an appeal to the Incarnation: —if in Christ God has assumed human form, this form is thereby essentially endowed with Power. Man portrays God in human guise, then, not as a mere makeshift and because he knows not the form of God, but precisely because he does know it, in Christ."[4]

So although images of gods and goddesses concretize in sensuous form that which is precisely without sense-content they may, within a given religious tradition, be entirely appropriate.

Still what the devotee sees as a metamorphosis the iconoclast or the upholder of negative theology judges to be a distortion. And yet as a Tertullian might put it: it is the very absurdity of worshipping an image that creates its power to evoke a religious response.

Notes

1. Gerald James Larson, Pratapadiya Pal, and Rebecca P. Gowen, *In Her Image: The Great Goddess in Indian Asia and The Madonna in Christian Culture* (Santa Barbara: UCSB Art Museum, 1980), p. 69.

2. Curt Maury, *Folk Origins of Indian Art* (New York and London: Columbia University Press, 1969), p. 54.

3. Rosemary Radford Ruether, *Sexism and God-Talk: Toward a Feminist Theology* (Boston: Beacon Press, 1983), p. 47.

4. G. van der Leeuw, *Religion in Essence and Manifestation*, trans. J. E. Turner (Princeton: Princeton University Press, 1986), p. 453. Originally published in German in 1933 as *Phänomenologie der Religion*.

Faith

Faith-*in*, we are often told, is an attitude that everyone has with respect to some central value or concern in their lives: faith in the importance and the possibility of acquiring positive knowledge, for the scientist; faith in the basic goodness of one's fellow human beings, for the moralist; faith in the rightness of one's country, for the patriot; faith in the skill of one's doctor, for the patient....Faith here is trust and hope: faith is the confidence that the truth, the good, will triumph. "Man would rather believe in Nothing than have nothing to believe in."

Religious faith, in its initial form, is of the same sort as general faith-*in*—with this exception, that it does not necessarily entail, although it may involve, having a set of "beliefs." Ordinary faith-*in* does imply some kind of belief that can be expressed propositionally. "Belief" today (but not always in the past; for example, in Old English "to believe" meant "to hold dear") indeed means some kind of intellectual assent to a statement or set of propositions; religious belief having the further characteristic, it is usually thought, of one's not having, or one's not ever being able to have, sufficient evidence to support one's assent to those propositions. Knowledge, as "justified true belief," therefore is ruled out with regard to the religious and is replaced by dogma.

But religious faith-*in* is not so much a claim about what the truth is, as it is an intense commitment to realize what one is spontaneously drawn to. Religious faith-*in* involves an openness, a sensitivity, and points the way toward that love informed by knowledge which imparts a joyful affirmation.

Faith, then, is not an attitude one assumes in the face of absurdity; faith is not a blind leap from darkness to a further darkness; faith is not an acceptance of a call that demands that one suspend the ethical; faith is rather the quiet assurance that one is becoming what one ought to be and the possession of the power to so become.

There is, then, an initial faith, constituted by trust and confidence that enables one to undertake solitude and to have the resolve to attain wisdom. To lack that initial religious faith-*in* is to condemn oneself to enduring all the vagaries of ego-based finitude.

And there is a consummatory faith that is entirely spiritual in character. Consummatory faith is an enduring, not an episodic, affirmation. It is grounded in the knowledge of one's existential historicity and one's essential spirituality.

Whereas the initial faith is a faith-*in*, consummatory faith is a faith-*of*. It is more of an assurance than a hope; it is that which enables one to see and to live in the realization of truth.

The faith with which one begins is thus taken-up and transformed in the faith with which one returns.

Part 4

Letters

Letter to a Colleague: On Religion and Good Taste

Dear Reverend Snowcroft:

I am grateful to you for sending me a copy of your review of my recent work. The good things you say are, of course, judicious and wise; the unhappy things are, naturally, something else! In your review you offer some very insightful observations of your own on the state of religion in the world and raise the question as to why today so many educated and sensitive people are "turned off" by most religious beliefs and practices. I would suggest that one answer might be that the exercise of those beliefs and practices do not conform to the dictates of good taste. Let me explain—and I welcome most warmly your critical response.

Good taste in both art and in life looks for harmony among otherwise discordant elements. It wants refinement, but with strength; structures informed with playfulness; seriousness, but without earnestness. It wants most of all to avoid the garish, the horrid, the merely extravagant.

Good taste abhors the uncontrolled, for it recognizes that when it is present, form is lost.

Good taste, in short, relies upon an adherence to appropriate limits of belief and practice. And good taste is inherently judgmental.

Unsurprisingly, then, good taste finds repugnant the emotionality of the evangelical preacher; the irrationality of

119

"speaking in tongues"; the unrestricted fantasy which peoples the heavens and hells of most religions; self-flagellations; fanatical devotion to saints; statues that weep; satanic sacrifices; drug-induced altered states of mind; oracles; holy wars; missionary zeal. These are all examples of excess which disclose a disregard for quality in virtue of their sheer extravagance.

It is, I believe, considerations of this sort rather than simple rational-scientific attitudes about religion that prevent most educated and sensitive persons from embracing, let alone appreciating, any of the religions of the world as generally practiced. It is the sheer vulgarity of so much of religion that good taste finds repulsive.

But, one might ask, would religion not be deprived of its "motivating power" (in Geertz's sense) if its excess were denied? Would religion then become a domesticated affair no different from other forms of entertainment, lacking depth and intensity? Doesn't the application of criteria of good taste to religion run the risk that we would all become Episcopalians?

The answer, I think, must be that a person of good taste is precisely one who is sensitive to what is appropriate in thought and behavior, the appropriate having to do with internal rightness and not conventional conformity. Good taste demands a right proportion between affect and situation, and shows the way for the attainment of genuine depth and intensity. Good taste, in other words, points the way for religion to attain a rightness appropriate to itself. And curiously enough, those who reject religion on grounds other than good taste often themselves exhibit a fanaticism which would be equally condemned by those of good taste. The will to disbelieve by the ardent atheist is often in its blindness of a kind with that of the most devout theist.

And so, my dear colleague, let us turn the whole matter in a positive direction and seek ways in which our religious life might be an exemplar of good taste. Let us strive to achieve style in religion as well as in all other areas of our life.

I eagerly await your response.

Yours faithfully,

Letter to a Former Student: On Creation

Dear Mr. Hotchkiss:

So you want to write a book—your first—on the idea of God the Creator, and you ask me my thoughts on the matter. Well, let me say straightaway that you should by all means write your book, and I hope it will indeed be highly creative. Personally, as I thought you knew, I am not much interested in "Creation" except as it relates to creativity, for I cannot ascribe to the usual theistic assumptions that God is a "first principle"; that creation is essentially causal in character (God the first cause, the world the effect); that there is some kind of absolute beginning (whether *in* or *with* time), and so on. I much prefer what might be a kind of Buddhist response to Heidegger's "fundamental question of metaphysics"— "Why is there something instead of nothing?"—to wit that the question ought rather to be "Why does something appear to be when in fact there is only nothing (*śūnyatā*)?" But more of that in a moment. Back to theism.

Paul Tillich, as you might recall, held that "the doctrine of creation [*creatio ex nihilo*] is not the story of an event which took place "once upon a time." It is the basic description of the relation between God and the world" (*Systematic Theology*, vol. I, p. 252). Creation, in short, accounts for human creatureliness; it discloses our ultimate dependency and incompleteness.

Now I think this existential-like approach has the merit at least of not pretending to be an explanation of the world (and one that could be set in opposition to one or another scientific cosmology), but that it still is burdened with many of those fundamental theistic assumptions which I find difficult to appreciate—and that it is burdened further with the theistic concern for finding an ultimate meaning in that human history that is subsequent to the creator god's handiwork. This concern, it seems to me, all too frequently becomes both a theological and existential obsession to discover some kind of principle by which we can attach some deep significance to our little lives. I much prefer the idea of being liberated altogether from this search for meaning and thereby attaining a genuine creative, and joyously playful, state of being.

Whitehead, as you know, is not easy to understand in these matters, but I think we can sympathetically resonate with his intent when he argues that "God and the World are the contrasted opposites in terms of which Creativity achieves its supreme task of transforming disjoined multiplicity, with its diversities in opposition, into concrescent unity, with its diversities in contrast" (*Process and Reality*, p. 528).

Creation as "Creativity" is not essentially cosmogonic insofar as it need not assume an absolute beginning; in fact, it finds most congenial the idea of beginninglessness, which in turn points in the direction of some kind of continuous creation—the self-giving, as it were, of spirit as a process, not as an event, which knows nothing of the temporal as such.

The question, then, is what would a non-theistic, spiritual account of creation as creativity look like and what bearing might this account have on one's religious life. To make a long story short, as the saying goes:

If in the last analysis there *is* only the One, then creation must be a kind of illusion, a making apparent of what lacks ultimate reality. But creation then becomes at the same time an illusion-making process that is utterly self-conscious, as it were, of being so—and hence creativity, a divine play, an expression of power for its own sake.

Creation would then disclose the freedom, rather than merely the dependency, of the "creature," for divine creativity would be an emanational extension of divine being and would thus set forth the possibility of a community of spiritually autonomous beings. Creatures would be as artworks, at least in their essential possibility. Creation would give the opportunity to a person to become right for itself and would set an essential, but not a universal, standard by which that rightness may be determined in its concrete particularity. In the end, then, creation would be found most intimately within oneself, indeed as oneself, and not in a causal relation between what we call the natural and the supernatural. Divine creativity, the supreme illusion, would open up a space for that free play of the spirit that we essentially are.

Well I don't know if any of this makes sense to you, but as your former teacher I can only advise you not to read too many theology books if that reading prevents you from discovering for yourself the living reality of divine creativity.

I wish you all the best.

Yours faithfully,

Letter to an Anthropologist:
On Truth and Archaic Religion

Dear Professor Bozesteen:

I appreciate very much your sending me the materials on "primitive religion" that you recommend I study. But what an abundance! You anthropologists have certainly been busy. Over the years I have, of course, read several things by you and your colleagues but I never realized how extensive and highly detailed the research was that has been carried out. From a philosophical point of view, I liked in particular the work of E. E. Evans-Prichard (namely, his *Theories of Primitive Religion*) and that of Wilhelm Dupré (his *Religion in Primitive Cultures: A Study in Ethnophilosophy*): the former for his solid common sense and erudition; the latter for his deep hermeneutical understanding and exploration. Both authors—and you, naturally, also—exhibit, it seems to me, a salutary sophistication in the very use of the term "primitive," which is a welcome relief from older anthropological usages with its fierce presumption of the superiority of the "civilized." In Evans-Prichard's words:

> Some people today find it embarrassing to hear peoples described as primitives or natives, and even more so to hear them spoken of as savages....But the words are used by me in what Weber calls a value-

free sense, and they are etymologically unobjection-
able. In any case, the use of the word 'primitive' to
describe peoples living in small-scale societies with a
simple material culture and lacking literature is too
firmly established to be eliminated. (p. 18)

Nevertheless, Dupré's remark that "primitive religion
has to be understood as the truth of religion with respect to
its initial integration into the cultural process" (p. 35),
suggests to me that, following Eliade, one might be better
informed by using the term 'archaic' rather than 'primitive,'
for 'archaic' gives prominence to temporal origins rather
than to anything structurally inferior and allows, as John
Hick points out, the inclusion of "both the 'primal,' 'pre-
literate' or 'primitive' religions of stone-age humanity and
the now extinct priestly and often national religions of the
ancient Near East and Egypt, Greece and Rome, India and
China" (*The Interpretation of Religion: Human Responses to
the Transcendent*, p. 23). In any event, subsequent to
studying a good deal of the material you so kindly sent, for
the question that concerns me most, I prefer to use 'archaic'
rather than 'primitive'.

Dupré refers to "the truth of religion with respect to its
integration into the cultural process." Now the matter of
"truth" is precisely what I want to discuss with you; but I
can't help but note how rarely that term—or concern with
it—appears in anthropological work. Indeed, Clifford Geertz
in his well-known collection of essays *The Interpretation of
Cultures*, offers and then unpacks a definition of religion as:
"(1) a system of symbols which acts to (2) establish powerful,
pervasive, and long-lasting moods and motivations in men
by (3) formulating conceptions of a general order of existence
and (4) clothing these conceptions with such an aura of
factuality that (5) the moods and motivations seem uniquely
realistic" (p. 90).

From this definition, and the entire manner in which
"religion" is understood by Geertz, religion is something that

happens only to others; the anthropologist standing outside
of it and so able to regard it as a "system of symbols"—the
"scientific perspective" self-imposing, he says, limitations
which preclude *"the hardly unimportant questions of whether
this or that religious assertion is true, this or that religious
experience genuine, or whether true religious assertions and
genuine religious experiences are possible at all"* (p. 123,
italics mine). But these are the questions—are they not?—
that go to the heart not just of "philosophy of religion" in
contrast to an "anthropology of religion" but to the living religious consciousness of any reflective person.

So let us discuss "truth and archaic religion" neither as
professional philosophers nor as scientific anthropologists
but as persons closer to "the religious consciousness of any
reflective person."

One difficulty, which is perhaps insurmountable, that I
think we must acknowledge from the outset, however, when
talking about truth and archaic religion is how to isolate
meaningfully any singular primal experience, idea or ritual
practice from the entire web of beliefs of which it is a part.
Dupré allows that "we have to understand it ["primitivity"]
as a *total interrelation* with respect to the symbolic culture
and members of the group" (pp. 25–26) and further that "the
inner-cultural circle of hermeneutics means that each
cultural fact has to be seen in the context of the whole
culture in which it is functional" (p. 30). It would seem, then,
that one cannot isolate for analysis of its truth-value any
primal idea or practice without having to take into account
its whole cultural matrix.

But if Jung is at all correct in asserting that "every civilized human being, whatever his conscious development, is
still an archaic man at the deeper levels of his psyche"
(*Modern Man in Search of a Soul*, p. 126), then perhaps we
can obviate the difficulty considerably by looking to some of
those archaic elements that can be said to be true for us
today and thus are part of our "total interrelation" with our
culture, of which presumably we have greater access and

understanding. We need move then from questions regarding the truth *of* the archaic to those regarding truth *and* the archaic as we find the latter still within ourselves.

It is not, however, I believe, necessary for us to look to Freudian/Jungian fantasy-like landscapes of the unconscious, with their ancestral heritages, archetypal symbols, instinctual drives for incest and cannibalism and the rest in order to address the issue. There is quite enough of the archaic available to us closer to the immediacy of everyday waking consciousness.

One of the key features of archaic consciousness, according to Eliade, as you will recall, is the recognition that the temporal and spatial are not indifferent serial or geometric orders *in* which happenings take place but are qualitatively differentiated in terms of the significance of various places and events that occur, some of which become sacred in virtue of the enormity of that significance. Certain places "center" the world for the archaic; certain events or rituals periodically performed re-create that very world.

And what a richer world it is when time and space themselves take on qualitative differentiation as they determine the right when and where (*kairos*) of human actions. We don't have to believe in astrology (although, if our daily newspapers are any indication, isn't it amazing how many of us still do?) in order to recognize the insufficiency of mere *chronos* in our experience. And if there is any validity in the notion that truth itself is a kind of rightness (rather than mere correspondence or coherence) then all the more closely are truth and the archaic aligned with regard to the temporal and spatial; for actions, when seen to be informed by *kairos*, become essentially performances—and they are thus seen to be true precisely in terms of their rightness, their creative articulation of meaning within the constraints of the situation. Whereas *homo faber* might well be a doer, *homo religiosus* is most certainly a performer; with his or her performance generating its own significance as well as deriving it from the way things happen in the world.

Henri Bergson, as you know, nicely criticized Lévy-Brühl's notion that "primitive mentality" was a kind of *sui generis* undeveloped rationality that attributed all manner of "mystic causes" to account for why certain things happened on the grounds that the "primitive" knew quite well that ordinary daily events are part of a causal nexus of regularity and that the other explanatory mode is appropriate only for those happenings of special human concern. Bergson quotes Lévy-Brühl: "Our daily activity implies unruffled, perfect confidence in the invariability of natural laws. The attitude of mind in primitive man is very different. To him the nature amid which he lives presents itself under an entirely different aspect. All things and all creatures therein are involved in a network of mystic participations and exclusions" (*La Mentalité primitive*, pp. 17–18). Bergson then goes on to observe that

> one point strikes us at once: namely, that in all the cases instanced, the effect reported, which is attributed by primitive man to an occult cause, is an event concerning man, more particularly an accident to a man, more specifically still a man's death or illness.
>
> ...We are not told that the primitive man who sees a tree bending in the wind or the shingle rolled up by a wave...imagines the intervention of anything more than what we call mechanical causality. The constant relation between the antecedent and the consequent, both of which he perceives, cannot fail to impress him: it satisfies him in this case, and, so far as we know, he does not here superimpose, much less substitute, a "mystic" causality.

Bergson then asks:

> When the primitive man turns to a mystic cause for the explanation of death, illness or any other accident,

what exactly is the process that he goes through? He sees, for instance, that a man has been killed by a fragment of rock dislodged during a gale. Does he deny that the rock was already split, that the wind loosened the stone, that the blow cracked the skull? Obviously not. He notes, as we do, the operation of these proximate causes. Why then does he bring in a "mystic cause," such as the will of a spirit or witch-doctor, to set it up as the principal cause?... What the primitive man explains here by a "supernatural" cause is not the physical effect, it is its *human significance*, it is its importance to man, and more especially to a particular man, the one who was crushed by the stone.

(*The Two Sources of Morality and Religion*, pp. 144–45)

I have quoted Bergson at some length, for apart from the sheer pleasure in doing so (whatever has happened to French *philosophe* writing since his time?), he has, it seems to me, made a central point which impacts directly on my question of truth and the archaic; namely, that truth has less to do with the semantic and more to do with the axiological; which is to say, that even for us today what is most fundamental for our experience, the persistent archaic, involves the existential significance to be had in our actions (and how we are affected by other actions and natural happenings) rather than indifferent causal connectedness as such. We worry about semantic meaning—and its truth as correspondence—when we utter propositions or statements; we care about existential significance—and its truth as rightness—when we justify and make sense of our experience. In short: we exhibit the archaic within us whenever we are intent on looking for, finding or creating an *irreducible* meaning and value in our lives—which presumably, going back to Geertz, is one way by which "religion" itself gets defined.

Well, please take these "initial" thoughts on the subject not as pronouncements but as invitations for further conversation. I eagerly await your reply—and thanks once more for your consideration in sending me some of the works of yours and your colleagues.

I remain, as ever
Yours sincerely,

Letter to a Visitor: On Religion and Humor

Dear Karuna:

My wife and I enjoyed very much your short visit with us, and thank you for your very gracious "thank you" note. You mentioned there, as well as during our lunch together, where we got on to so many different topics, your wonderment about the relation between religion and humor. You rightly pointed out that for most people, especially in the West, religion is a deeply solemn affair. Indeed, think of a Jonathan Edwards or a modern evangelical preacher; although to many of us fit subjects for comedy, to themselves and their followers they appear to be dedicated solely to the serious business of salvation.

Now in every religion there have been "holy fools" who don't quite seem to know how to navigate in this world and who exhibit all the cross-purpose kinds of action which we associate with the comic, but it is, it seems, only in the polytheistic, on the one hand, and the nondualistic, on the other, that genuine humor is fully intended in and by those modes of consciousness.

Polytheism, in any of its embodiments, already has a number of playful gods, for instance, your own Hindu Bālakṛṣṇa, to amuse and delight their devotees, gods that perform all manner of pranks and appeal nicely to a kind of universal folk humor. Symbolizing as they do so clearly the

131

entire range of human action, it is no surprise that the doings of the gods express all the *rasas* from the heroic and the erotic to the humorous.

With the non-dualistic, a very different situation, I think, obtains (albeit, the pluralistic and the non-dualistic, as you know so well, are often aligned in a given tradition as a whole), for with enlightenment there is that very release from obsessive concern for saving one's soul and the attaining of that awareness of absurdity which informs genuine humor at its core. The Taoist master, the Zen monk, a Ramakrishna, an accomplished Hasidic rabbi, know of this and fill the heavens with their laughter. As well they should.

Well we need to meet again soon and explore this whole topic together at leisure. Some time ago I read a very good article on "Humor in Zen Buddhism" but I have forgotten who wrote it or where it was published. But you can imagine what it said.

All the best,

Letter to a Layman: Animadversions
on Natural Theology

Dear Mrs. Fielding:

I very much appreciate receiving yours of the 5th. You write to me, you say, as a layman "concerned" (forgive my saying so, but I also got the impression that "obsessed" would not be inappropriate) with the enterprise of proving the existence of God. You seem to be well informed about the traditional proofs, whether of an ontological, cosmological, or teleological sort, and with much of the relentless criticism that has been directed against them, whether on the big scale ("all such proofs assume what they allegedly prove," "'existence' is not a predicate," "'necessary existence' is a contradiction in terms") or in little ways ("'greater than' is vague," "even in an infinite time not all possibilities need be realized"). Nevertheless, as you note, there has been an extraordinary amount of interest exhibited of late in the proofs and this interest has led at least one observer (a Mr. J. Donnelly in *The Review of Metaphysics* 26, no. 1, p. 159) to note that "A new natural theology is abroad in the land."

But before the pious rejoice, I think it might be useful to recall the words of Kierkegaard that "if God does not exist it would of course be impossible to prove it; and if he does exist it would be folly to attempt it," and, in this spirit, to look at the religious dynamics of this proof-making enterprise to see what in fact its relevance for the religious life might be.

I suggest we might begin by asking, What does it mean to *think* the existence of God? St. Anselm, in his famous ontological argument for the existence of God, made much of the notion that all men understand what 'God' means, and then argued that "we think of a thing, in one sense, when we think of the word that signifies it, and in another sense, when we understand the very thing itself. Thus, in the first sense God can be thought of as non-existent, but in the second sense this is quite impossible. For no one who understands what God is can think that God does not exist" (see his *Proslogion*, chapter 4). Anselm, it would seem, is thus arguing that when we understand what God is (in contrast to what 'God' means) we must think his existence and we cannot think his non-existence. Now the distinction he draws here between thinking about the word and thinking about the thing that is signified is, I believe, important. As St. Thomas Aquinas rightly pointed out in his criticism of the ontological argument, "we do not know the essence of God" and therefore "the proposition [asserting his existence or the impossibility of his non-existence] is not self-evident to us" (*Summa Theologica*, third article).

For our purposes, ontological thinking (as distinct from image-making) can, I think, be defined as that mental activity which, through the use of signs/symbols (words) recognizes and establishes relationships between known entities. By this definition one cannot think ontologically without knowing the objects of one's thought, for without such knowledge one would not have a basis or "locus" from which relationships could be determined. And to know the object of one's thought means to experience or to have experienced it precisely as an object to one. Is it not the case, then, that ontological thinking is necessarily rational-empirical— that it must involve a subject/object knowledge by acquaintance? Anselm is right, I think, in his manner of recognizing this, but he is wrong in thinking that this favors his argument; for as God cannot be known as an *object* neither he nor his existence or non-existence can be thought.

Ontological thinking implies separation from what is thought; and, in religious terms, it fortifies separation. To *think about* God in the context of *a priori* proof-making means to think about the word, and this word-thinking, it seems to me, neither brings the full reality of God to mind as a positive content of consciousness nor can it properly lead to any truly rational convincement concerning his existence.

Another way of looking at this might be to suggest that all proofs (*a priori* and *a posteriori*) for the existence of God start from a position that is antithetical to religious consciousness, if they assume a problematic status to the Divine. What is problematic for religious consciousness is not God but the world. For genuine theistic faith and insight "God" is the most assured of all realities. It is the status of the world that is in doubt. How can it be real in the presence of the overwhelming reality of spirit? That, and not the existence of God, is perhaps the question for religious consciousness.

Let us suppose, however, that a proof for the existence of God withstood all criticism and was rationally convincing. What consequences would this have for religious living?

When the question is put this way we sense immediately (do we not?) that the answer is "very little, if any." The "God" that would be proven, we rightly sense, is only a bare concept; it is not a spiritual reality that is or may be a content of consciousness.

Who would undergo a radical self-transformation on the basis of a rational proof? Religious commitment, experience seems convincingly to show, arises from either direct experiential insight, from "non-rational" contemplative and loving experience, or from the more shadowy but none the less powerful "irrational" depths of our instinctual being. A "decision for religion," whatever that might mean, is not like a choice between two or more near-at-hand realizable courses of action which are to be carried out for the purpose of satisfying some specifiable end. To speak even of choosing religion or of deciding on making a religious commitment is indeed, in spite of William James' idea of a "will to believe," an odd way of speaking. It assumes a rational voluntariness that is simply missing. It would actually be closer to the felt-actualities of experience to speak of being chosen (see, for example, in the Indian Vedāntic tradition the *Kaṭha Upaniṣad* I, 2, 23, where it is stated that he who attains spiritual insight is chosen), although this too might be misleading if it suggests that someone else or a god is doing the choosing for one.

But the religious dynamics of proving God's existence, of natural theology, is not, assuredly, exhausted by these negative factors concerning the thinkability of God's existence (the separation of the ontological thinker) the un-genuineness in religious terms of the consciousness so involved in taking the existence of God as problematic, or the lack of efficacy of even a successful proof, were one possible, for there are, it seems, several positive aspects of the enterprise which must be noted, and especially since they seem to point in a direction quite different from what would be anticipated by the monotheistic proof-maker.

Critics of the traditional proofs for the existence of God (namely of Thomas' own five proofs), as you know, often point out that what the proofs actually establish, if they establish anything at all, are various aspects or attributes of God—his surpassing greatness, his goodness, his perfection. And herein, I think, lies one of the positive features of proof-making: a proof may articulate dimensions of spiritual life for notice and response.

As a first step away from a self-assured and facile naturalism, which so many of us find congenial, an *a posteriori* proof may be formative of consciousness in its leading it in the direction of spiritual reality. The mind becomes what it thinks; that is to say, mental dispositions are formed in terms of the content of one's thought. The making of, as well as close study of, a proof may set one in the direction of religious consciousness. When "perfection," for example, is put forward in a proof as being of the essence of God's nature one's consciousness may be altered by the recognition of the possibility of this perfection. The self may thus be confronted with an ideal toward which it may strive and in terms of which it may measure its own actions and attitudes.

But, and here is the curious conclusion we are lead to, natural theology then goes to show the desirability, if not necessity, of *polytheism*—for the aspects and attributes of divinity that various proofs might call attention to are numerous and multiform. There are many, if there any, manifestations of spiritual life. Various functions may be ascribed to the Divine —loving kindness, creativity, perfection, care—which call for different responses. When one exhibits reverence one is doing so not toward God as absolute reality but toward him or her as identified with one or more functions or attributes, that is toward God as a god—and in this way one is seeking a path to the Godhead.

And why should there not be *many* paths? There are many different types of persons, intellectually, emotionally, spiritually—and any one person's life-story usually tells of very different kinds of needs and interests that are operative at different times in one's life. Diversity is the natural condition of life and this plurality (of objects, values, ideas, ideals) can be spiritualized best through a rich variety of approaches and beliefs.

Gods, and not God, as David Hume once noted, are the proper objects of religious consciousness as brought forth by natural theology.

I hope this conclusion is not upsetting to you, but if it is I suppose it could always be argued that the many attributes of divine being always require a single unified center in order for them to be attributes (if I recall correctly the theologian Robert Neville once argued for this rather forcefully) and hence monotheism once again; but this all turns on rather obscure and very difficult questions concerning the nature of the Divine and not his or her existence as such.

Well, my thanks again for writing to me and I warmly welcome your response to these "Animadversions on Natural Theology" which were prompted by your thoughtful letter.

Most cordially,

Letter to a Concerned Scholar:
On Religion and Morality

Dear Dr. Henry Worth:

I have been reflecting on the comment you made recently at our Association meeting that no one seems to take seriously anymore the relation that once was thought to be so intimate between religion and morality; indeed a relation so close that not long ago for many persons "religion" meant morality as much, if not more than, it meant intense forms of private spiritual experience. The situation, it seems to me, if I may continue the conversation with you, is quite complex, reflecting as it does both profound social changes where everything concerning morality has been questioned and differences in fundamental types of experience that have been able to re-assert themselves with the breakdown of the religious monopoly of orthodox theism.

Spiritual consciousness, in what many of us take to be its highest enlightened form, allows that divine reality is "beyond good and evil," which is to say that the categories "good" and "evil" do not apply to reality, being, as they are, modes of human judgement derived from our worldly experience wherein we seek—and sometimes attain but more often than not are frustrated in our striving to attain—the fulfillment of various needs and desires. Where there is no ego, so it is said, there is no moral judgement. When oneness obtains, so it is

138

argued, differences are obliterated. Everything is thus at once equally valuable and valueless from the standpoint of that which is of surpassing worth—the content of enlightenment.

Archaic consciousness, on the other hand, which is re-appearing today in so many new forms, is concerned not so much with spiritual insight and completeness, but with over-coming defilement and attaining purity, whether as an experientially attained possession or as a ritualistically given beneficence. Purity here obviously does not mean some kind of chastity; it means rather, as I understand it, some-thing like a literal cleansing of the soul, a washing away or a burning away of all one's accumulated "bad karma." Annihil-ating one's private demons, conquering the living night-mares of consciousness, one strives to stand in a pristine space which allows a new beginning.

Morality here becomes then a search for innocence—the re-attaining of (what we now believe was erroneously thought to be) the simplicity of the very young. The accumu-lated impotence of experience is to be set aside: one is to be renewed.

> Yet here's a spot.
> Out, damned spot! out, I say!
> What, will these hands ne'er be clean?
> Here's the smell of blood still: all the perfumes
>   of Arabia will not sweeten this little hand.

Children in the Judeo-Christian tradition, and no doubt in other theistic traditions as well, are taught—are they not?—that "nothing is hidden from God." This is intended, it would seem, not as a theory of perception but as a claim of moral judgement. Every human act, thought and desire is measured under the imperatives of divine commandment. *Conscience*, then, emerges: the internal voice of pain and reward, of remorse and approval.

Moral consciousness for theism then seems to take two principal forms: (1) the awareness of sin, together with the hope for redemption, and (2) the sensitivity to moral value in human action. The two forms, for most of us, are not apparently connected.

Man as sinner: the awareness of finitude, of our turning away from the divine. Sin as pride, the substituting of our little selves for Him from whom we derive and have our being. To sin, originally or otherwise, is to deny in practice our spiritual being. The awareness of sin is thus said to imply the awareness of that within us which always retains its purity and worth.

On the other hand, ethical consciousness, we have come to believe, has most fundamentally to do with the developing of a sensitivity to that which promotes and exhibits human dignity. Rights and virtues might be extolled, but they have their reality only as they set forth a quality derived from that deeper sensitivity. Kindness, generosity, care and concern are spontaneous; they are neither calculated nor utterly fortuitous—and, and this might be the main connection between the awareness of sin and ethical consciousness, being spontaneous they necessarily reflect that retention of moral worth which grounds our very being.

And so, it seems to me, the main task of "religion and morality" is to reconcile, or otherwise re-organize the relations between, the enlightened, the primal, and the theistic. And you, my good friend, with your deep understanding of all of these forms of religious life, would seem to be ideally qualified to do this—and so I hope you will accept your appointed task and best wishes for the success of your work!

Yours,

Part 5

Definitions and Poems

Words

grace

Grace is the right reception of spirit. Spirit is always giving; but it is seldom received rightly.

To receive spirit rightly means that we be available to it in spirit. It is spirit which welcomes spirit. Grace is not an intervention of the pure into the muddy; it is rather the return of the self to its spiritual ground. It is the self that makes the movement, while thinking "I am selected."

Grace is a gift of spirit: but only for one who doesn't need it too strongly to receive it.

happiness

Many are the reasons
        for sadness.
The source of happiness
        is one.

humility

Humility is the acknowledgement that the only real being one has is the presence of the divine.

worship

How can we who never worship know what it means to measure ourselves vividly against what we think He is, and find ourselves utterly wanting? Worship is not the positive recognition of surpassing qualities in the object adored, for this recognition, if it took place, would be enlightening—and with enlightenment there is no differentiation. If He were there as presence we would not be there to worship Him.

vulnerability

Temples at Nara: the warriors in stone guard the deity as though he were vulnerable.

Vulnerability as a religious category: the divine condition, the human tragedy.

heaven

Having the power to obliterate, selectively, one's past, as though karma did not obtain.

But then only a part of oneself would be present and able to listen.

sin

Does a consciousness of sin mean only that one has caught a glimmer of a qualitatively different state of being? Is it possible that sin has nothing to do with the moral or ethical and only with the ontological? But then why would anyone be driven by an awareness of it to such intensities of remorse and despair?

compassion

Compassion, *karunā*, flows from freedom and cannot be present without freedom. When one is not free one expects to take as well as to give. One must be free from self, from ignorance, before one can be free to love.

forgiveness

To forgive someone their sins is easy so long as one has not been their victim. When as a victim, however, to forgive is not so much a way of dealing with another person as with oneself. Forgiving as a victim means to refuse to allow one's own pain and suffering to make one revengeful and rageful and thereby self-destructive. One's tormentor has truly won if one ends up defeating oneself.

perfection

One life is sufficient to realize perfection, and no life is sufficient which fails to realize it.

guruship

Is it really the case that someone can know "me" (one's requirements for salvation, for *mokṣa*) better than one can know oneself?

Is it from weakness or from great strength that one turns oneself over to another in total obedience?

the personal

The spiritual problem: to transform a supreme impersonal truth into a personality or into a personal realization.

distances

Religious consciousness is often a sensitivity to the *distance* between the human and the divine. Created by a withdrawing ego, the distance is then justified as the work of a creator god.

conversion

Conversion involves a moral transformation; but it is not just a matter of putting off an old self and taking on a new one; rather it is the becoming of a person who is no longer even capable of recognizing the old.

separation

Separation is more than being "apart from;" for to be separated means to have the potentiality to be "united with" or to be "close to." To be aware of being "apart from" is to acknowledge difference; to be aware of being separated is to recognize similarity.

loyalty

Religions claim that one must be unconditionally loyal to the Divine. All other loyalties and attachments (to family, friends, causes, institutions) are partial and revocable; and are indeed to be revoked when they prevent or prohibit absolute loyalty to the Divine.

The claim is extraordinary; as its fulfillment calls for the greatest possible courage and devotion.

dukkha

Is ecstasy too a kind of "suffering" because it is not perdurable?

Pain is "physical" while suffering is "mental." One has a pain or "that is painful," but "I am suffering." Where there is no ego there is no suffering—although there might be pain.

Pain, we are told, does perform needed biological functions (signaling physical deterioration and the like). The problem is to determine the spiritual value of suffering.

reality

The unreal is that which cannot be intuited. Only that which is a content of intuition is real; only that which is when the subject/object distinction is obliterated is fully real.

names

Concepts become names when the realities to which they refer have experiential origins.

To coin new words is not necessarily a sign of profundity or originality. Most often it is merely the gathering of old errors around new sounds.

recognition

Spiritual knowledge is not so much a cognitive activity which involves a manipulation of abstractions, as it is a state of recognition. One knows something spiritually when one is aware of it as a self-possession. Spiritual knowledge, as distinct from empirical, analytical, scientific knowing, is thus essentially self-knowledge.

problems
Humans are not so much problem-solving creatures as they are problem-creating creatures. After a certain stage in development, we create problems in order to have something to do. Activity breeds activity, and so the wheel turns.

the devil
The devil is where and when sterility, anguish, and rage reside.

sacrifice
Sacrifice is the giving up of the unreal for the real. It is the turning of oneself over to the Divine. Rejecting the world as unmeaningfully given, it is the affirming of a spiritual ground to being. To sacrifice means to preserve a continuity with the Holy. It is entirely a mental-spiritual activity when it is what it should be.

anticipations
No anticipations ought to stand between the self and reality.

mystery
A mystery, although unintelligible in principle to us, is entirely luminous to itself.

Claiming us as its own, it is terrifying only when, confronting it, we retain our intellect and treat it as a problem to be solved.

When participating in it, a mystery becomes simply our living reality.

In the last analysis, then, there is only the utter mystery of being.

the path
To return properly is, in its own way, more difficult than to go rightly.

Three Women in Religious Art

Redon's *Mystery*

Mystery is pervasive. In silence it broods upon and plays within the vibrant forms, the greens and blues, the luminous yellow. Have they a source, a meaning, a place within the infinite twilight that surrounds them, and with which she feels an affinity, an unconsummated unity?

She feels the presence of herself and of things growing that are unfulfilled. She knows that all things are in Him, and that He is nothing and is everything in His own plenitude.

She is bathed in the silence of spirit. The ubiquitous silence whose serene white light glows within all things. She is a woman and the woman within her knows itself truly only by its relation to a pervasive mystery.

Bernini's *Saint Teresa in Ecstasy*

To receive she suffers and knows the meaning of pain. Her body is buried beneath flowing folds; still, in rapture, she turns toward Him.

There is within her silence and humility, or is there only love and joy? Her silence is eternal. Her love is everlasting. She believes that woman transfigures the spiritual in man.

Fra Angelico's *Annunciation* (Prado)

Equal before her kneeling announcer, careful to guard her sacred treasure, at the moment she knows what it is to receive. Her arms are crossed. She leans forward and accepts the golden light. O wondrous gift of spirit! O light emerging from light and pure whiteness!

Does she know? Draped as the star-dotted blue. Does she know from the written word? An angel is telling her something in silence. He will die, ascend to the whiteness, and be declared the Lord. Eve and Adam are expelled from the garden, and in fear they protect each other.

She feels nothing. Only wonder. For the woman within her knows it must be as nothing in order to beget Him.

They Call It a Home

Old, too old for being
There, sleeping and groaning
Unaware
Of how old the cycle is
That brings them
To their beginning.

Still
They call it a home
Where alive
Death is a blessing to all.

Memory and Time

We bear too many memories to walk
quietly in the winter-still woods
where a river runs
recklessly, looking for weak spots
to flow in its ice-worn world.

❦

Clear blue sky
Single flower
Not lonely.

❦

We who tirelessly sit
among shadowing trees
Know what time is
and how it gets its way
When we fail to listen
now and then.

DATE DUE

			Printed In USA